THE BIG LIFE OF
Little Richard

ALSO BY MARK RIBOWSKY

THE BIG LIFE OF
Little Richard

MARK RIBOWSKY

DIVERSION
BOOKS

For more information, email info@diversionbooks.com

Diversion Books
A division of Diversion Publishing Corp.
www.diversionbooks.com

First Diversion Books edition, August 2020
Hardcover ISBN: 978-1-63576-722-3
eBook ISBN: 978-1-63576-723-0

Printed in The United States of America

1   3   5   7   9   10   8   6   4   2

Library of Congress cataloging-in-publication data is available on file.

CONTENTS

CONTENTS

[He] was brash, fast and bombastic . . . . He wore a baggy suit with elephant trousers, 26 inches at the bottoms, and he had his hair back-combed in a monstrous plume like a fountain. Then he had a little toothbrush moustache and a round, totally ecstatic face. He'd scream and scream and scream. He had a freak voice, tireless, hysterical, completely indestructible, and he never in his life sang at anything lower than an enraged bull-like roar. On every phrase he'd embroider with squeals, rasps, siren whoops. His stamina, his drive were limitless and his songs were mostly non-songs, nothing but bedrock twelve-bars with playroom lyrics, but he'd still put them across as if every last syllable was liquid gold.

—NIK COHN,

Awopbopaloobop Alopbamboom: The Golden Age of Rock

The music was new black polished chrome and it came over the summer like liquid night.

—JIM MORRISON,

on Little Richard's recording of "Rip It Up"

JUST RHYTHM AND BLUES, PLAYED FAST

On May 9, 2020, Richard Wayne Penniman's incredibly bristling life ended the way his songs never did: fading out in peace and quietude. After eighty-seven years of rhythm, blues, rock and roll, and mayhem, the otherworldly dynamic force known as Little Richard was where he wanted to be: in his home in Tullahoma, in southern Tennessee, where he had found paradise lost in the hills seventy-seven miles down Highway 41 from the Nashville clubs where he had once cut his teeth and where he'd performed, without a second of peace or quietude, a repertoire of sound and fury—one song in particular seeming even then to gush from his soul the loudest. It was a song—a groove—created from the disjointed, confused tapestry of a troubled youth, and sixty-five years later *still* gushes from the soul of rock and roll. This is what a timeless song can do. It spans what seems like eternity.

This song wore a title as outlandish as Little Richard's wardrobe.

"Tutti Frutti."

* * *

WHEN LITTLE RICHARD got to New Orleans in September 1955 to make his first recordings at J&M Studios for Specialty Records, label president Art Rupe and producer Robert "Bumps" Blackwell had replaced his regular backing band, the Upsetters, with the same sidemen who backed Fats Domino and Lloyd Price on their J&M recordings.

Some of the industry's most famous side men, in fact—Lee Allen on tenor sax, Alvin "Red" Tyler on baritone sax, Earl Palmer on drums. Justin Adams and Edgar Blanchard on guitar, Frank Fields on bass, Huey "Piano" Smith (who would be a star himself, fronting his band the Clowns) and Mel Dowden on keyboards. They were, as Blackwell said, "the best in New Orleans," gathered to play behind a singer they had never heard of, and whom they cackled about behind their instruments.

"They all thought I was crazy," Richard looked back. "Didn't know what to make of me. They thought I was a kook."

Blackwell, who had arranged the charts for the eight sides Richard would record, had himself not met the artist at the hub of the session until just before it began. Little Richard ambled into the room—as Blackwell recalled, "this cat in this loud shirt, with hair waxed up six inches above his head" who was "talking wild, thinking up stuff just to be different. I could tell he was a mega-personality." No matter his bona fides, or lack thereof, Richard came in calling the shots, or so he thought. He was memorable, that's for sure. But when he practically took over the session, demanding authority, the result was so shoddy that, in the booth, Blackwell never saw fit to turn on the tape machine.

He, like the musicians, sensed that Richard—for all his bravado and craziness—was fighting himself: "I had heard that Richard's stage act was really wild, but in the studio that day he was very inhibited. Possibly his ego was pushing him to show his spiritual feeling." Blackwell added, "If you look like Tarzan and sound like Mickey Mouse it just doesn't work out . . . . I didn't know what to do. I couldn't go back to Rupe with the material. [There was] nothing to merchandise. And I was paying out serious money."

Both he and Richard felt deflated as they and Lee Allen retreated to an in-crowd club called the Dew Drop Inn to drink away the blues and find a new groove. As it happened, it would come as if riding a lightning bolt. At the Dew Drop, Richard lost whatever inhibition he had. Getting up on the stage, in his element as bar-goers crowded in front of him, he sat at a piano—or rather, stood above it—and launched into a song he had been performing live for months, but never figured would be acceptable for recording. The first sounds of it were those beguiling syllables that came out as *Awop bop a loo mop a good goddamn / Tutti Frutti, good booty.*

This, the original parlance of "Tutti Frutti," had entered his head back where he worked in the kitchen at the Macon Greyhound station during a misspent youth, giggling to himself as he wrote the leering lines about "good booty" and "If it don't fit don't force it / You can grease it, make it easy." Up on a stage, he paid no mind to good taste. He just let it rip. And as he did that, Blackwell was astonished. It was as if the song liberated Richard from the circumspect Richard in the studio. He had swagger, bark and bite, his joy and his growl emanating from a place deep in his soul. He was a different breed of cat, claws out, answerable to any standard of R&B, only himself, with not a compromise in sight.

Having heard the first clarion calls of rock and roll, the song was his entry into a side room of R&B where things ran at a quickened pace. Richard himself would one day boil rock down to being "just rhythm and blues, played fast." And so, right from that bombastic opening of "Tutti Frutti," leading right into his hammerhead piano triplets, it was the quintessence of the new order. Bumps was sold, recalling, "I said, 'Wow! That's what I want from you, Richard. That's a hit!'"

Again, as a metaphor of life itself, nothing is that easy in rock. There was a hitch: those all-too-obviously obscene lyrics needed delicate editing. But Bumps was right. Oh, was he right. The song had the seeds of rhythm and blues, jazz, bebop, but its beat was stronger, the lyrics geared to teenagers needing to adopt a new cultural mode as their own. So much so that the case can be made that when Little Richard recorded "Tutti Frutti," it marked the functional birth of rock and roll.

one

PRETTIEST THING
IN THE KITCHEN

Look anywhere . . . I am the only thing left. I *am* the beautiful Little
Richard from way down in Macon, Georgia. You know Otis Redding
is from there, and James Brown's from there . . . . I was the best
lookin' one so I left there first. Prettiest thing in the kitchen, yes sir!

—LITTLE RICHARD, 1970

Little Richard began his life blessed by fate, which took the
form of a clerical error. On December 5, 1932, a nurse in a
Macon, Georgia, hospital filled out his birth certificate, but she'd
misheard the name that his parents, Charles and Leva Mae Penniman, had chosen for him—"Ricardo Wayne Penniman." The nurse
scribbled "Richard Wayne Penniman" on the certificate. And when
Charles and Leva Mae saw it, they thought it sounded better than

Ricardo and left it alone. But for that moment of acceptance, their son may have had to transform rock and roll as Little Ricardo.

The third child and second son of Charles, who everyone called "Bud," and his young wife, whom he had married at age 14, Richard Wayne came home to roost in the Pleasant Hill section of Macon, squarely in the middle of Georgia, ninety miles from Atlanta, a strategic location that made Macon the chief supply depot for the Confederate army during the Civil War. Its topography was lined with the neatly manicured remnants of antebellum plantation society, and during Reconstruction those fields of cotton had become a magnet for freed slaves working as sharecroppers. The city called itself "the prettiest and busiest city in Georgia," a measure of the civic pride its residents had in a place where segregation, and periodic lynchings, were a hard reality but integration a real actuality, found daily in the downtown core of the city. Here, enterprising black men stoked a teeming hub of nightclubs and speakeasies that became a vibrant musical scene, one that would incubate some of the greatest talent of the century.

The Pennimans lived a few miles to the north, in a cramped, one-story house with a yellow exterior at 1540 Fifth Avenue, sitting on a hairpin-turn corner of Middle Street. Unpaved, and not what a visitor would call luxurious, the streets of Pleasant Hill *felt* as such to the residents—a suburban-like nexus of roads where the trees were leafy, the air breathable, the lawns mowed. Of his formative years here, Little Richard would recall, "We weren't a poor family and we weren't a rich family." And never were they destitute. Bud, who didn't let moss grow under his shoes, made sure of that. He was not an educated man—though his wife came from a family of well-schooled, wealthy people—but he made it his business to succeed. No saint, a bit of a cad, Bud was possessed of a too-hot temper, yet he made his minister daddy proud by becoming a preacher, herding his brood to church on Sunday, where he launched into fiery sermons that had the parishioners stomping, screaming, and singing, one of the first rituals of life that Richard immediately warmed to.

Bud worked long hours as a stone mason while also bootlegging booze for Prohibition-era moonshiners around town, rationalizing that he wasn't committing a sin because he didn't brew the stuff himself. After booze was relegalized a year after Richard was born, Bud still ran moonshine to merchants who didn't want to pay tax on their liquor supplies. His son would recall seeing shady-looking guys in the house and sometimes cops waiting outside the front door. The influence of music in Macon was such that music was in the air even for bootleggers. One, Richard remembered, would sit around the house playing a washboard. And Bud, having avoided any serious scrapes with the law, in time earned enough money to buy a nightclub downtown, the Tip In Inn. Like almost all the clubs in the red-light district centered on Fourth Street (later renamed Martin Luther King Boulevard), it was a "black and tan" bar, catering to both races. The receipts helped pay for Bud's snazzy Model-T Ford and household luxuries such as electric lamps, the envy of neighbors who still made do with gas lamps. The Pennimans could even afford a nanny to help Leva Mae with the kids, as the brood kept growing to twelve: seven boys, five girls.

Richard was, like Leva Mae, fair-skinned, his sharp facial features faintly Native American, as were those of many of his maternal relatives. He was quite striking and rambunctious, drawing the wrath of his mother, whom he adored and would praise for her "inner strength" while describing Bud with left-handed praise as "a very independent man," not willing to define what he meant. Clearly, Richard was closer to Leva Mae, who seemed far more tolerant of his congenital physical flaws and personal *quirks*. For one thing, his right leg was shorter than the left, forcing him to walk with a limp and a shuffle. He also, he said, "had this great big head and little body, and I had one big eye and one little eye." Richard himself would use words like "crippled" and "deformed," the slurs he heard as the target of schoolyard taunts. Given that his walk made him seem effeminate, "the kids would call me faggot, sissy, freak, punk. They called me everything." But he didn't seem to go out of his way to dispute the slurs. Indeed, he played up his feminine affectations, even creeping into Leva Mae's room and painting his face with her makeup and dousing himself with her rosewater perfume. He would imitate her speech, in a girlish, high-pitched voice.

She would just shake her head. Bud, on the other hand, would, like most who encountered Richard, ask out loud, "What's wrong with that boy?" The answer would have been complicated, too complicated—perhaps—for those times and that place. Instead, when the boy would act out and get himself into trouble, Bud would administer a swift whipping with his belt. Richard would take it, then go right back out wearing his makeup, perfume, and effeminate mannerisms. In time, things would only get more complicated, and strained, between father and son, as Richard seemed to represent everything Bud detested. Richard admitted years later that "I knew I was different from the other boys" and freely spoke of the "unnatural" urges he had for the boys much like him. He even admitted to indulging in acts of homosexuality. He mentioned a particular ritual in Macon, of young blacks on the corner picked up by white men in cars and spirited into the woods for sex, hoping to be given some money. Within the borders of a culture where lynchings were all too common and "White" and "Colored" signs hung on restaurant doors, some black men submitted to this behavior as a means of survival. Richard was one of them.

He seemed curiously amenable to living on dare, bravado, and tightrope danger. Often goaded into a fight by other kids, he would wind up with his pretty face bloodied. At those times, his big brother Charles would intervene. "If I found out they had messed with Richard," he said, "I would go looking for them." Richard had a mouth that kept roaring, whether singing or not, and would "get on our nerves hollerin' and beating on tin cans. People around would get upset with him yelling and screaming. They'd shout at him, 'Shut up yo' mouth, boy!' and he would run off laughing all over." In many ways, he was already Little Richard, precocious, able to create a ruckus, and aware of how valuable his vocal cords would be. It gave him a sense of purpose to inject himself into youthful gospel-singing groups that spilled out of the churches onto the streets. The first that he could remember was called the Tiny Tots, led by a matronly woman he knew as Ma Sweetie. There was also one unit composed of two of his younger brothers, Marquette and Walter, and Richard himself. Named or not, the bands would sing on the streets, on people's porches for fruit and candy, sometimes even for a few bucks.

"It was really somethin'," he once said. "Everybody be singin'. We would be washin' [clothes] in the backyard, just singin' and we sound like a big choir, and we never practiced: it was a big choir like fifty voices all over the neighborhood."

Sometimes, his uncle Willard would drive them out to small country towns where the pay was a little better, places like Logtown (Bud's hometown), Forsyth, and Perry, to perform at summer camps and churches. The songs included "Precious Lord" and "Peace in the Valley." Richard became so immersed in singing that his school studies suffered. He contemplated dropping out to pursue a career in the clubs, but the thought of what Bud would do stopped him; nor would he even play hooky. "I had the kind of father," he said, "that would kill you if you did that. He would have knocked my head off with a switch."

THE WRATH OF Bud, in fact, was more and more a growing undercurrent of his life as he reached his teens during the bleak years of World War II, when many young men in Pleasant Hill were gone with the draft or enlisted into segregated Army units. Even as he acted out in ways Bud fretted about, Richard sincerely believed he might become a preacher, knowing his father would approve. Indeed, he thought he could have his religion and sing it, too. One of his early influences was Brother Joe May, the singing evangelist billed as "the Thunderbolt of the Middle West." May, also born in a town called Macon, in Mississippi, was not an actual preacher but his tours ignited black audiences, such that one writer described him as "the greatest male soloist in the history of gospel music." May would sell millions of gospel records, but none until 1949 when he cut "Search Me Lord." Richard caught one of his shows at the Macon City Auditorium and saw his own future.

As it was, Richard was spending most of his time in one church or another, since his parents each belonged to different congregations, Bud to the Methodist Foundation Templar, Leva Mae the New Hope Baptist. He also bounced around to other churches where three of his uncles were ministers, and several more in the neighborhood, singing in the choir. Already, he had become hip to having a shtick along with a voice. When he was just 10, he remembered, he would "go around saying I was a healer. I would go to people who were sick and I'd sing gospels and touch them, and a lot of them would *swear* they felt better! They gave me money sometimes."

Then came the changing winds of blues and R&B. Among the myriad of influences Richard would look back on, he cited the great Louis Jordan, the "King of the Juke Box" of the swing era, a tornado of talent who sang, danced, led his band, and blew his horn, all loudly and at warp speed. Jordan was not only heard but seen on movie screens in "soundies" that Richard would sit and watch for hours in Macon theaters. One of Jordan's R&B hits, "Caldonia," was the first non-church song Richard said he ever sang, and it was no accident that Little Richard's song titles were women's names—a common trait in Jordan works.

Although he never was able to pay enough attention in school to be a decent student, when he went to Hudson High School he was taught to play the alto saxophone and joined the school band. Horns were the basis of jazz and R&B compositions, and it made Richard more serious about music as a calling. The Macon City Auditorium and some of the grittier downtown clubs were important stops on the underground circuit of secular-based blues wailers, and Richard became a habitué crisscrossing the downtown streets, inhaling the vibe, the scent, the sound of what would soon congeal as a new idiom—rock and roll. Downtown Macon not only nurtured the black roots of rock, but also Emmett Miller, a white minstrel performer whose piercing falsetto sounded a lot like Richard's and traced back to the yodeling component of hillbilly music.

Whatever the strain of music one could groove on, there was an undeniable reach for something beyond the limits of conventionality. And if there was anyone who originally set free these emotions, it was young black singers and musicians who, one by one, streamed through the clubs and, when they could take a step up, the Douglass Theatre, founded by Macon's first black millionaire, Charles Douglass. The marquees had names like Hot Lips Page, Cootie Williams, Lucky Millinder, and Richard's favorite singer, Sister Rosetta

Tharpe, who sang while playing a guitar. These were transitional figures, alloying the music of the Lord with devilish, hip-grinding blues rhythms and open appeals to affairs of the flesh. Of them all, it was Sister Rosetta who flourished the most; years later, she would be given much credit for pioneering rock and roll, and retro-dubbed "the original soul sister." Despite taking flak from black churches, she never wavered. Rare for a black woman, she recorded for a major label in the '40s, Decca, ringing up R&B hits with bluesy versions of spirituals like "Strange Things Happening Every Day."

Today, these songs are notable for their primordial, chugging "rock beat," fusing her loud resonator guitar (today known as a dobro), piano, bass, and drum. Back then, to a teenager seeking musical nirvana, Sister Rosetta playing the Auditorium was so enticing that Richard took a job there selling Coca-Cola just so that he could wait at the stage door for her to arrive. When she did, he boldly strode up to Rosetta and sang "Strange Things." Impressed, she invited him to sing on stage that night, to hearty applause. It was, he said, "the best thing that had ever happened to me." Indeed, not only did Sister Rosetta press forty dollars into his hand afterward, he now had access to the building and other acts. One was the great Marion Williams, who fronted the immensely popular gospel/blues Ward Singers. Her contribution to his assets was more essential. As he said, "She was the one I got that Whoooo! from."

BY 1949, SEVENTEEN-YEAR-OLD Richard was something of a novelty on the fringes of "race music." He was able to jam with any act that came through the clubs. If he felt it, he'd jump up on the stage. He did this with a performer known as Doctor Nobilio, the so-called "Macon town prophet," who was decked out in a red-and-yellow cape and turban, waving a magic wand and carrying a gruesome doll he said was a devil baby with claws for feet and horns on its head. Richard would also hook up with a touring group called Dr. Hudson's Medicine Show, the leader of which actually sold snake oil from the stage. That took him out of Georgia for the first time, to play dates in Florida. He still only knew a few non-gospel songs, but he could scream louder than anyone else. That scream earned him other road gigs, during which, unable to pay even for a room in a fleabag hotel, he would plop down in a field and sleep there. Even on the best of days, navigating the landscape of the Deep South was filled with routine peril.

"I used to get beaten up for nothing," he once said. "Slapped in my face with sticks. The police used to stop me and make me wash my face. I always tried to not let it bother me. We could stay in no hotels and go to no toilets. I went to the bathroom behind a tree. I slept in my car. I knew there was a better way and that the King of Kings would show it to me. I was God's child. I knew God would open that door."

And if not God, then folks who gave him shelter. In a hick Georgia town called Fitzgerald, Ethel Wynnes, who owned a nightclub there, "took pity on me," he recalled, feeding him "chitterlings and pigfeet." And when the front man of a band called B. Brown and His Orchestra got stone cold drunk and couldn't make a gig at her club, Richard stood in, then went off on another tour of the hinterlands, with *them*. Of such fortuitous turns of fate is history made. It was on those treks that B. Brown had him go by the stage name "Little Richard," even painting the appellation as the band's featured performer on the side of the Bingo Long-like station wagon they traveled in. It stuck. Man, would it stick.

As breaks go it wasn't much, but it at least epoxied him to the bubbling sediment of postwar race music, which was getting more vibrant—and louder—all the time. Delirium suited Little Richard just fine. The more of an exhibitionist he could be, the better. Sometimes, he would sing the standards, or fake it, knowing just a few words of "Goodnight Irene" and "Mona Lisa," but that was paying dues, marking time, until he could detonate. He was clearly on the move but still picking up affectations from other acts. He could see that the saxophone was for backup musicians, not the singers. But the piano could be a useful prop; a man could sing while tickling the keys with a flourish, rise from the bench and play upright, bounce around, lead the band. And so he enlisted a local piano player, Luke Gonder, to show him the basics, while developing moves such as lifting his foot to the keyboard and sliding his hand under it to play.

But therein was the rub, at least for Bud. At the Tip In Inn, his roster of acts and the selections on his jukebox were strictly mainstream pop and blues, the soothing sounds of Duke Ellington, Ella Fitzgerald, Louis Armstrong, the Mills Brothers, Bing Crosby, the Andrews Sisters, and the like. In Bud's judgment, mainstream blues/jazz such as "Take the A-Train," "Lulu's Back in Town," and "Boogie-Woogie Bugle Boy of Company B" were about as funky as he would permit. Whenever his son would sing at a competing club, Bud thought of him as part of the new crowd of euphoric blues busters, wearing the same sort of flashy suits, shaking and rattling, boasting of carnal pursuits—the very essence of the devil's music. That his boy was a teenage wunderkind did not impress him. Already feeling shamed by his son's irreverence, Bud boiled over.

"My father didn't like loud music and I dressed loud [too] so he put me outdoors when I was 13. He didn't like me because I was gay. He'd say, 'My father had seven sons and I wanted seven sons. You've spoiled it, you're only half a son.' And then he'd hit me. But I couldn't help it. That was the way I was."

In truth, Richard had already been on the street for some time, and quite accustomed to finding a bed or bench wherever he could. The night Bud evicted him, he floated downtown, to one of his haunts, Miss Ann's Tic Toc Lounge, owned by "Miss" Ann Howard and her husband Johnny. This was a natural magnet for Richard, as the clientele was, well, everybody—black, white, straight, gay (before long it would become Macon's first openly gay bar). As he recalled, he jumped up on stage and sang, "and the people went mad. I played this song called 'Guitar Rag' on the piano, and I used to have to play that four or five times a night. So they adopted me and [later on] bought me a brand new car, and I went to school, and she was just like my mother for many years. Then Johnny passed away, and I got famous, but she wouldn't ever take any money from me, I [still] offer her money, but she won't take it. They are millionaires, themselves, but they were really sweet to me. I slept in the same bed between them and I'll never forget them."

His highest words of praise for anyone were reserved for them: "I think they had a lot to do with me being Little Richard."

After school, he would roll into the Tic Toc, father and son avoiding each other though just steps apart. He'd wash dishes for a few dollars, hang around, then squeeze into a seam in the evening shows to belt out a few songs to the delight of the gay patrons. He would also make mental notes for songs he would begin writing, in the kitchen, after sitting at tables with strangers and making himself comfortable, two of them in-progress versions of "Long Tall Sally" and "Miss Ann." About the first song, he recalled there was "a lady who used to drink quite a bit, she always like pretend she had a cold when she came to our house . . . and she was tall and ugly, man, that was an ugly woman. She was so ugly that people used to turn their heads, she didn't have but two teeth and they were on each side of her tongue, and she was cockeyed. So we used to say, 'Long Tall Sally, she's built for speed,' and her old man they called John.

"In Georgia, when you're raised around a lot of people, you call them your uncle and your aunt, so we used to call this cat Uncle John, but he was really married to Mary, which was a big, fat lady, who used to sit on the porch and eat watermelon all the time . . . . All the black people got paid off on Friday, and you'd know when Friday came, because of whiskey and fights and joyful times, too, and she and he started a good fight. So when he'd see her coming, he'd duck back in this little alley."

Another song that formed in his head came from watching his Aunt Lula unwittingly get high on weed, the result of a practical joke by the family. "They used to slip grass in her pipe [and] put tobacco on top," he said. "She'd puff away. She didn't know what was happenin', she just be laughin' . . . she was a little lady, she didn't have teeth; she'd swing almost over the rim. That's where I got the idea for 'Good Golly, Miss Molly,' somethin' she used to say when she got high swinging up there. Everything I sang was really something that happened."

IN HIS LATE teens, he was maturing as a quite handsome young man, with no gawkiness, growing to nearly six feet, lean as a two-by-four, his cheekbones carved high, enabling his smile under his pencil mustache to explode across his face. He wore his hair in the manner many of the race music singers did, in a mile-high, pomade-contoured pompadour, which he had done years before but appeased Bud by cutting it short. His swagger was more than cute; it reached into an audience and demanded their attention. He owned the room. And even Bud had to give in to the reality that his boy was going to go his own way, singing his own music. When Richard dropped out of Hudson High, both Leva Mae and Bud knew they couldn't convince him otherwise. The irony was that Bud would actually grow closer to his son once he wasn't under his thumb anymore. The two of them would begin an uneasy reconciliation process, with Bud making what for him was a major concession coming to see him sing. To Bud, it behooved them both that Richard fend for himself, be a man.

"He has a phone number," he told Leva Mae. "And if anything should happen, he can always call and we'll come and get him. We'll be right here." His final words on the subject were succinct.

"Let him go," he said.

In truth, he was already gone. For good.

two

AIN'T NOTHIN' HAPPENING

I tried to take voice lessons, but I found I couldn't because the way I sing, a voice teacher can't deal with it. I'm out of control. True singers, people who know something about music, not rock and roll, have told me there is something special there. I thank the Lord for it. Once I hear a song, I wish I were singing it! The music just makes my toes and my hair move!
—LITTLE RICHARD

As the new decade dawned, the newly christened Little Richard still had a way to go before becoming a star. He'd need to endure some difficult interludes during which he was perilously close to giving up, crawling back to 1540 Fifth, and studying for the ministry. The minimal money he pocketed for gigs with the groups that streamed through town could suffice when there were patrons who would foot his bills, some expecting favors. As he lurched toward his twenties, he wasn't quite the same prize. And so he had to

take menial jobs to make ends meet. Still, he was able to keep claw-
ing his way up, by inches, not miles, in the music world. After the
B. Brown band gig was over, he latched on with a minstrel show
headed by one "Sugarfoot Sam from Alabam." History records that,
for this run, Little Richard was in drag.

"One of the girls was missing one night," he related, "and they
put me in a red evening gown. I was the biggest mess you ever saw.
They called me Princess Lavonne."

Unable to walk in high heels, he merely stood in place as the
audience of predominantly gay men guffawed at what Richard
would admittedly call "the freak of the year." And while he decided
to split from Sugarfoot Sam, treading on the gay underground
earned him a reputation and more gigs with similar acts more concerned with pandering to gay sensibilities than advancing gospel or
rhythm and blues. Among these outfits were the King Brothers Cir-
cus, the Tidy Jolly Steppers, and the L.J. Heath Show. For most of
them, Richard had to put on a dress again, with makeup and red
eyelashes, and camp it up. It did not seem to be a ticket to ride, but
it surely was a ticket out of Macon, putting him on the back roads
and big inner cities of Georgia and Alabama. And, being in the
crosscurrents of a bustling superhighway of black talent, both high
and low level, he was making connections that would bring him his
first real break.

He bounced to another traveling band, the Broadway Follies, a
burlesque show of gay singers, dancers, and comedians, which was
operated by a guy named Snake and whose headliner was a drag
queen called Madame Kilroy. When Richard began with them, one
of the performers was Atlanta R&B singer Chuck Willis, six years
Richard's senior and still paying *his* dues—which, in a roundabout
irony, would come to fruition after Richard had altered the musical
landscape and Willis scored a massive crossover hit with a juiced-up

cover of Ma Rainey's blues ballad "C.C. Rider." Both of these future shining stars were on the way up, but still waiting for opportunity to knock. For Richard, there was a crucial connection made when the Broadway Follies moved into an Atlanta club called Bailey's 81 Theater, a big-time venue that regularly attracted top-billed blues men like B.B. King and Jimmy Witherspoon, who had recording contracts and toured nationally. Seeing them perform was a dose of reality for Richard, who believed the crowd reaction he would receive meant he too was a star, until they came on and the house shook.

But being able to hang with them opened another door, when he was introduced to Billy Wright, a jump blues wailer who bore a remarkable resemblance to Richard Penniman. While the Atlanta-raised Wright gave his birth year as 1932, same as Richard's, he was clearly much older, though his past was murky. What was known was that he was a trip, having made his mark in the blues clubs as a female impersonator. Calling himself the "Prince of the Blues," he wore slathered-on makeup, loud suits, hair piled atop his head, and a pencil mustache. He didn't sing the blues as much as squeal them. In the late '40s, having become the house act at Atlanta's Royal Peacock Club, Wright recorded some of his first songs right there at the venue for the Savoy label, his first release, "Blues for My Baby," reaching number 3 on the R&B chart. According to Richard, Wright's mixture of showbiz flair with gospel and blues wailing and weeping was an epiphany.

"He really enthused my whole life," he would say. "I thought he was the most fantastic entertainer I had ever seen."

Wright had a circle of pet acts that he pulled strings for. And Richard wasn't only good; he was a smart social climber. Knowing how to appeal to Billy, he began to imitate him, his face covered in the same makeup as Billy, called Pancake 32, and singing Wright's songs in tribute. Wright noticed. By 1951, he had a small set of sycophants around Atlanta, and Richard quickly became another one, gaining real benefits. Billy touted him to a disc jockey named Zenas Sears at Atlanta blues radio station WGST, where Wright and other local big-label blues singers recorded. To Richard's surprise, Sears quickly secured him a contract with RCA Victor Records. The company was a real giant, its sales strategy based on being the largest manufacturer of Victrolas. And on Victrolas, people often played records also made by RCA, especially the seven-inch, 45-RPM disc invented for single-song plays, making obsolete the old 78-RPM long-play discs. (Columbia, the largest American record label, invented the long-play, 33 1/3 disc, originally for symphony orchestra music.)

Once recorded, the discs made at WGST under the provenance of the artist's label would be plugged by Sears on the air, an arrangement that no doubt included under-the-table "payola" bribes for Sears, a common facet of the industry then, and often the only way a "race record" could get air play. Even a huge corporation like RCA, unlike Decca, Okeh, Atlantic, and Savoy, was slow to get into the R&B market, and not until 1953 would it found a sub-label for it. The company solons in New York's Rockefeller Center gave little attention to blues or jazz, ceding major talent to other labels. Even so, the contract given to Richard Penniman was not materially different than those commonly extended to black talent: a commitment for eight sides with limited sales runs and a royalty of a half-cent for each record sold. This was typical—and would be for decades—for even some highly successful black (and white) artists, who leaped at the chance to get in a studio, a reward all its own. Few made any money at all, some victims of avaricious, fly-by-night managers who preyed on young, naive men desperate for a break. In 1951, Little Richard was one of them.

*　　*　　*

TWO MONTHS SHY of his nineteenth birthday, Richard Wayne Penniman could legally sign a contract without approval from either Bud or Leva Mae. He did so and on October 16, 1951, entered the WGST studio for his very first session, or any singing gig not before an audience. The session, paid for by RCA, would produce the first four sides under the auspices of an RCA staff producer, with Richard, who also played the piano, backed by Billy Wright's band. The songs chosen for Richard were something out of the Wright playbook. The first cut, "Get Rich Quick," was one of two songs written by British blues composer Leonard Feather, a jump-'n'-jive number with Richard singing/shouting above red-hot sax solos by Albert Dobbins—a track that, heard now, qualifies as sheer rock and roll. The other Feather track, "Taxi Blues," was in the same mold but bluesier. By contrast, two songs written by Richard were blues ballads, "Every Hour" and "Why Did You Leave Me," turning him into a formulaic torch singer, the key too high, making his voice crackle and perch on the border between sounding sexually ambivalent, either male or female.

There was an earful here, yet little of it was riveting. Oddly, Richard sounds older on these tracks than he would half a century later, restrained to the point that the songs sound as if recorded at a slower speed; in retrospect, the lack of audience heat and the plodding pace of a studio session probably kept the vibe way too tame. Of them all, the suits at RCA saw the most potential in "Taxi Blues," releasing it in November under the name of Little Richard with the RCA catalog number 47-4392. "Every Hour" was the B-side. Played first over the airwaves by Zenas Sears (of course), the A-side failed to rouse the station's listeners, sending Richard back to his usual grind playing in the clubs. Then the DJ flipped the record over and "Every Hour" made some noise, prompting Wright to quickly step on Richard's moment, cutting the song himself. While Richard's original version received little air play outside Georgia, he was stunned when he heard it played on a station in Nashville, screaming, "That's my record!" Soon, the song had found its way into juke boxes around Macon and Atlanta—and one in particular that meant everything to Little Richard.

That was the record machine in Bud Penniman's club.

Bud now proudly bragged about his once-shunned son, and even dropped nickels in the box to keep playing the record. As Richard recalled, "My daddy was proud of me for the first time in his life." The pride came with the assumption that, while his son had breached the old man's rules singing the devil's music and adopting a perverse lifestyle, it was a vindication of sorts that the songs Richard had recorded were pretty much conventional rhythm and blues. That was enough for Bud to beckon Richard to return to the house on Fifth Avenue, the home he had been cast out of. The elder Penniman also began acting as his informal adviser. To Richard, this sudden rapprochement alone seemed to make the recordings worth it. He moved back in, son and father catching up on much lost time.

Soon, the local success of "Every Hour" prompted entertainment managers to learn the name Little Richard. One, Horace Edwards, who represented blues bassist Percy Welch and his orchestra, visited the Penniman house armed with a contract. Encouraged by Bud, Richard signed and was quickly back out on the road, doing one-nighters on the chitlin' circuit and in underground gay clubs.

He was making good pay, Welch giving him a hundred dollars a week, but his continuing education into the wild underside of the new rhythm and blues was priceless. Yet another influence was Eskew Reeder, an openly gay singer/pianist who like Billy Wright performed wearing makeup and billowy wigs, as well as cool wraparound shades, a soon-to-be mandatory rock and roll accessory. Richard was floored by Reeder's ability to pound the keyboard's highest notes and still create coherent melodies, driving up the vibe of delirious excitement. When Richard asked him how he did this, Reeder came to the house and taught him how on a portable keyboard.

In the long lens of history, people like that were but ships passing in a night that was just beginning for Little Richard. But they left a mark in his soul—and, ironically, he would in time ease the entry for many of them into the incipient rock and roll era. Welch, for instance, would record with his band under the name of Percy Welch and His House Rockers, achieving some success in 1957 with the suggestive "Back Door Man" (not to be confused with the more famous song of the same title by Willie Dixon). Reeder would record under the moniker Esquerita or the Magnificent Malochi, cutting such Little Richard-like tunes as "Hey Miss Lucy" and "Rockin' the Joint."

The wilder, louder blues bubbling along the chitlin' circuit were Richard's metier, but RCA had no stomach for it, keeping him in the safe corner of conventional blues and R&B. A second recording session was set up for January 1952, with RCA expecting more of the same from him. And, rather than looking forward to another round in the studio, Richard felt he was being misused and undersold. While moving up the ladder helped bridge the distance between him and his father, it did little for his confidence in his talent. Bud, he would say, "thought I was famous. But I wasn't." He felt aimless, unsure of himself, and if Bud approved, he fretted that perhaps God didn't.

*   *   *

THOSE MIXED EMOTIONS and inner discontent arrived with Richard at the WGST studio on January 12, 1952. And the songs he recorded that day are discomfiting, the titles seeming like they could have sprung from a session with a shrink—"I Brought It All On Myself," "Please Have Mercy On Me," "Ain't Nothin' Happening," and "Thinkin' 'Bout My Mother," though only the last was written by Richard. Of the others, one came from Leonard Feather, two from jazz/blues composers Howard Biggs and Joe Thomas, who had written for Jelly Roll Morton and were paving the way for '50s doo-wop harmony groups like the Ravens and the Beavers. (Biggs, too, would arrange the Silhouettes' "Get a Job," one of the biggest crossover hits of the '50s.)

Backed once more by Billy Wright's band, Richard's tracks were solid but much the same as before. Richard again sang in a low, bluesy key, with no flourishes or real fervor, the band likewise hitting no memorable peaks. To be sure, it was quite serviceable blues, and fascinating curios as stepping stones in Little Richard's oeuvre, though few would ever hear them after RCA released his second record in early February, the A-side "Get Rich Quick" from the first session, the B-side "Mother."

However, almost tauntingly, just as the wishfully titled "Get Rich Quick" went into the playlist rotation at WGST, Richard Penniman took a gut punch that would upend his life and test his faith for the first but not last time.

It happened on the night of February 12, 1952. That evening, the dashing, forty-one-year-old Bud Penniman was mingling with the clientele at the Tip In Inn when a strange incident interrupted the music and mingling at the bar. Hearing a series of loud, piercing bangs coming from the kitchen, he went to check it out and found a local punk named Frank Tanner—whom Richard years later would dubiously call his "best friend"—tossing firecrackers into an oven, setting them off one by one. Bud at first did no more than tell Tanner to stop, but when he kept on doing it Bud ordered him out of the club. On the outside sidewalk, Tanner joined some of his friends in harassing people going in and coming out. Flashing his famous temper, Bud reached into his waistband for the pistol he carried everywhere and ran out to the street, brandishing the gun. But as soon as he was through the door, Tanner, drawing his own handgun, pulled the trigger, sending Bud to the concrete with a bullet to the chest. In the commotion, cops arrived and arrested Tanner. An ambulance was called. But Bud Penniman was pronounced dead on the spot.

His son was on the road that night with Percy Welch and knew nothing of his father's death until he got home the next morning. Entering the house, he saw his father's blood-drenched raincoat lying on the ground on the front porch. Inside, Leva Mae, pregnant with her next child, was sobbing uncontrollably.

"Richard," she told him. "your daddy's dead. No more Daddy."

His knees began to buckle, in shock, then he straightened up and demanded to know what happened. When she told him that Bud had been murdered outside the Tip In Inn, full of rage, Richard wanted to know who had done it. She refused to say, fearing that her boy would go out looking for the killer and get himself killed, too. His sister Peggie had no such reservations. She had been at the club earlier that night, dancing with friends, to Richard's songs that Bud played on the juke box, and which may have been playing as Bud lay dying on the street. She left shortly before the shooting. When someone came to the house with the bad news, Peggie ran all the way back to the Tip In, blood in her eyes. By then, Tanner had claimed he acted in self-defense and was released. The Penniman family would never accept that excuse. Although Bud hadn't ever talked about it, the Pennimans weren't naive. They knew he was involved with some unsavory people, people who—if owed money—would not wait for it. Some of those people, they suspected, wore uniforms.

"We believe that someone had my daddy killed," Richard said years later, going on rather cryptically that "we were too poor [to] get a lawyer and fight it. We believe that the police didn't like him because . . . that's all I can say."

Bud's funeral was held on February 20, 1952, in the chapel at Hutchings Funeral Home, then he was laid in the ground at Linwood Cemetery, surrounded by his widow and their eleven children and dozens of friends, relatives, and possibly enemies. Then the brood he left to fend for themselves went back home, Leva Mae demonstrating the strength and stoicism that her son would fulsomely praise in interviews to the end of his life—the very qualities he had already memorialized quite presciently in the song that was on the market as Bud was laid to rest, "Thinkin' 'Bout My Mother," a sorrowful ballad that begins: "When I think about my mother / All I can do is cry."

Bud's murder was never fully investigated or resolved. It merely faded away, one more case of a guy with dubious associations overstepping the line. The postscript was that Frank Tanner was to be indicted for manslaughter, in June 1955, before the case was dismissed by the district attorney in October.

The Pennimans carried on, harboring no expectation that any of them would ever be rich or famous. Richard became the breadwinner when his brother Charles enlisted in the Marines and was shipped out to fight in the Korean War. The Tip In Inn, which never made much of a profit, was closed when Leva Mae couldn't keep it open. All she had to live on was around five hundred dollars that Bud had saved up. She used that to pay off the house and feed and clothe her children. She would soon remarry to a man named Enotris Johnson, raise more kids, and shepherd the family. And Richard exercised remarkable forgiveness for Frank Tanner. A decade or so later, after he had indeed become a quasar, both rich and famous, he was visiting the family at the house when Tanner showed up at the door, "asking us to forgive him."

Added Richard: "And we did."

FORGIVING OR NOT, Richard had to live with the verity that God had cruelly taken away the father whose acceptance he needed, and who had come around to believing in him. Bud was even going to buy him a car the next morning so he could travel to his gigs in style. The cruel fate that cut short Bud's life burrowed into his son's soul and his subconscious, leaving doubts about the tender mercy of the Lord, and whether the son's sacrilegious lifestyle somehow claimed Bud. Yet he carried on, under emotional duress, having to make it, needing to make it. As of 1953, the notion that he would succeed seemed shaky at best. The failure of "Get Rich Quick" only mocked him, more so when RCA put out its remaining Little Richard product in two more releases in May and November: the A-sides were the equally mocking "Ain't Nothin' Happenin'" and "Please Have Mercy On Me." (It would take until a 1958 retro album before all eight sides would be available on the budget RCA Camden label.) Neither disc was marketed or sold with any enthusiasm, and even Zenas Sears seemed to have moved past Little Richard.

By year's end, RCA's commitment to the aspiring artist was cut; the contract would not be renewed. Richard didn't pretend he had not failed; he admitted it. But he didn't wallow in self-pity either. If everyone else was giving up on him, he wouldn't. He was even optimistic enough to believe the Lord was on his side, sizing him up as a messenger, a music man/preacher. Though he would still regularly consider and reconsider going into the ministry, he kept it at bay while he went on singing in the clubs and assembling bits and pieces of songs to be written.

To be as confident as he was seemed a flight from reality. When the new year 1953 dawned in Macon, Richard was working as a dishwasher at the Greyhound bus terminal. Not because he *had* to, he insisted, but because he liked to sit in the terminal on his breaks and observe people streaming through, listening to the stories they told. According to one of the ever-revolving explanations he had for writing "Tutti Frutti," it was there in the terminal that he came up with the immortal intro that would become the subject of great academic debate for future generations.

"I was washing dishes at the Greyhound bus station at the time," he said. "I couldn't talk back to my boss man. He would bring all these pots back for me to wash, and one day I said, 'I've got to do something to stop this man bringing back all these pots to me to wash,' and I said, 'Awap bop a lup bop a wop bam boom, take 'em out!' and that's what I meant at the time. And so I wrote 'Tutti Frutti' in the kitchen, I wrote 'Good Golly, Miss Molly' in the kitchen, I wrote 'Long Tall Sally' in that kitchen."

Nobody really knows if that story was itself a riff. But one thing is certain: he was *hearing* the music he wanted to sing. What's more, he had the stones and the ego to push himself on people who could move him toward that end. Having rubbed elbows with nearly everyone in Macon who had any connection to the music scene, he regularly strode up to one or another and pitched himself, usually to be brushed off, until one day he lobbied Clint Brantley. A big-talking black man, Brantley had done well for himself. He owned another of the Fourth Street clubs, the Two Spot, promoted lucrative concerts at the Macon City Auditorium, and managed many of the acts that played his club. Although he seemed to be dismissive of black singers, calling them "little niggers," he was instrumental in their progression in the music business, giving them a stage and, if he saw an upside, becoming their manager—at a 50 percent commission. He could be generous, too, advancing performers for their performances as well as expense money, though exacting repayment with fat interest under threat of physical harm.

Brantley's pull was so strong that as integration progressed inch by inch in Macon, he dictated the forms it took. At his club, and also the Macon Auditorium, there were loose "white" and "colored" areas—but, twisting the realities of Dixie, it was the *whites* who sat behind the blacks; at the Auditorium, the white audience was concentrated in the balcony only, toward the rear, separated from the front, symbolically, by a rope. Clearly, Brantley was a man that few loved; but fewer wanted to rub him wrong. And yet, the person who could abide him least was the lever of power that unleashed the development of soul music. That was Little Richard, who eagerly agreed to Brantley's becoming his manager, though he suspected the two would eventually clash.

When Brantley took on Little Richard in 1953, he had of course known of Richard, whose duet with Sister Rosetta Tharpe in the Auditorium was considered one of the electric moments in that building. But Brantley had held off on trying to sign him as a client until he matured yet also proved that he could still sing as he did as a teenager. Of course, it had also been the case that Bud Penniman was acting as his son's de facto manager. Bud's death changed the equation. Not that Brantley saw much of an upside with Richard's RCA flop being a hurdle to overcome. The first thing he did was to put Richard on the road to build up a music-scene buzz and word of mouth.

"Get yourself a band," Brantley told him, "and there's plenty of work available."

AS IT HAPPENED, a band found *him*. When Brantley booked Richard for a gig at the New Era nightclub in Nashville, a five-strong outfit led by trumpeter Raymond Taylor, whose wife Mildred played the drums, were looking for a singer. Hearing the cat from Macon, they immediately offered the job to him. They named themselves the Tempo Toppers, and the next day were in New Orleans, playing the next Toppers' appearance, at the Dew Drop Inn. With no time to rehearse, or even get a suit for him that matched theirs, Richard took over as lead vocalist on the group's gospel/blues numbers, which were performed while one of the guys in the band performed feats of strength such as lifting a chair while someone sat in it. Yet Richard was, well, Richard: untamed, his sudden falsettos soaring in perfect pitch, his piano pyrotechnics and incandescent personality lighting the audiences up.

By now, the early roots of rock and roll had begun to set in the loam of the blues, in breakneck, free-form arrangements of repetitive hooks stabbing at the foot-stomping, piano-and-horn-driven rhythms punctuated by rumbling bass notes and crashing drums. And the Tempo Toppers, who also included Billy Brooks, Barry Lee Gilmore, and Jimmy Swann, could fit nicely into the formula, which Taylor applied when writing original songs for them. Those fortunate enough to witness and feel the raw revelatory might of Little Richard during this period would be able to say they saw the future of American music; on these jags through the South, his name carried heavy weight. Hamp Swain, a saxophonist, who had gone to high school with Richard before forming a big band called the Hamptones—and in 1954 would become Macon's first black disc jockey at radio station WBML—played many of the same clubs along the chitlin' circuit. He recalled that "whenever you said Little Richard was appearing, you could depend on a crowd—all through Georgia, Alabama, and Florida." In time, Richard would front Hamp's band, and both men, along with Clint Brantley, would nurture the almost dual rise of James Brown, preceding by a decade that of Otis Redding.

The thunderous reception in these joints opened a handsome income stream for Richard, a good bit of which he kept hid from Brantley, lest he be left with peanuts. It also opened the door to another record label when the Toppers played a date at Club Matinee in Houston. One of the town's biggest top cats of the black music scene, Don Robey, who owned the vibrant Duke-Peacock R&B label, was in the house—and was blown away by the front man's wild virtuoso performance, which he closed by intoning to the audience, "This is Little Richard, King of the Blues . . . and the Queen, too!" Robey had lined up a roster of bold young prototypical rock and roll acts for his label, including Clarence "Gatemouth" Brown, Memphis Slim, Floyd Dixon, the ill-fated Johnny Ace, and Big Mama Thornton, who later that year would score the gnarly "Hound Dog," which was produced by Los Angeles blues bandleader Johnny Otis.

A jack of all trades, Robey had been a gambler, taxi fleet owner, liquor salesman, and owner of the ritzy Bronze Peacock Club before turning it into a recording studio. He not only ran the label but also managed much of the talent on it, and wrote and published their songs. That is, he *claimed* he wrote them, using shady practices such as listing on the writers' credits fake names that allowed him to disburse royalties to himself. Much like Clint Brantley, his business was promoting black talent but uncomfortably for Richard, however, Robey was an all-too familiar character, a near twin of Brantley, a light-skinned black man who seemed highly scornful of "lesser" and darker black men than himself, freely meddling in their recordings with a my-way-or-the-highway attitude. Not bothering to consult Richard or the group, Brantley and Robey closed the deal, Brantley agreeing to the usual measly, half-a-cent artist royalty. By the time of the signing, the Taylors had branched off from the Toppers to form another band, the Deuces of Rhythm, with Richard at times singing for that group as well. Thus, because the Toppers would be recording three of Taylor's songs at the first Peacock session (one would be credited to Robey) and because Taylor and his wife would participate in the session, a compromise was made. The first record released would be credited to "Deuces of Rhythm and Tempo Toppers, Lead: 'Little Richard.'"

The recordings took place on February 25, 1953, at Robey's studio. The songs chosen each had neat hooks tied to current trends. "Ain't That Good News" reached deep into the pulpit, the title borrowed from a spiritual (as would the later Sam Cooke classic with the same title), and featured a tempo shift from languid to breezy blues. "Fool at the Wheel" joined in on the hot-rod craze of early rock, accelerating with deep bass strains and feverish choruses of "ba doo baah." "Rice, Red Beans and Turnip Greens" made a detour to throwback group harmony while injecting a slinky organ run. The lone Robey song, "Always," was the weakest, a more generic group harmony throwback.

As with the previous RCA work, all these songs had a certain charm—like Richard's standout high notes—but they lacked the wallop that Little Richard wreaked on a stage. The missing magic let down no one more than Richard himself. Still, he bridled when the songs were released—first "Ain't That Good News"/ "Fool at the Wheel," then, with Robey allowing the record to be credited to "Tempo Toppers, Featuring: 'Little Richard'," "Always"/ "Rice, Red Beans and Turnip Greens." With no promotion and sporadic air play, they sold few copies. Naturally this situation heightened the tension between he and Robey. As Richard would recall, Robey— who some in town called "the Black Caesar" and ran with a pack of heavily armed goons—was "almost like a dictator."

"He was a black guy who looked like a white guy," Richard continued, "and he was very stern. He wore great big diamond rings on his hand and he was always chewing this big cigar, cussin' at me . . . . He was so possessive. He would control the very breath that you breathed. I resented him for being so mean."

And Richard let it be known, telling the other acts that Robey was "rude" and "nasty," and "how he didn't pay me," and that he was a "crook" who "was just using all these people—using them up." Accordingly, he noticed, Robey "was very angry with me." The two of them argued often and eventually Robey blew his stack. During a set-to in his office, he leaped from his desk and came after Richard, who recalled the result. "He jumped on me, knocked me down, and kicked me in the stomach. It gave me a hernia that was painful for years. I had to have an operation. He was known for beating people up, though. He would beat everybody up but Big Mama Thornton. He was scared of her."

The timing of this explosion virtually ended the relationship. It came after Robey, conceding he couldn't get the best out of Richard, had prevailed on the ubiquitous Johnny Otis to produce a second round of recordings for the Tempo Toppers, conducting his own band behind the group. Otis, the son of Greek immigrants, who led his own popular blues/jazz band, was regarded as a keen judge of talent, having discovered Little Esther Phillips and Etta James, and had a string of R&B hits himself with his band, including "Double Crossing Blues" and "Cupid's Boogie." His discovery of Big Mama Thornton preceded the seismic release of "Hound Dog," which he produced, cowrote, and backed on drums.

Otis, who would be the caliph of a veritable R&B duchy in Northern California, with regular TV and radio shows, took a liking to Richard and brought him into Robey's studio on October 3 to cut four more sides, all written by Richard, backed by Otis's band and female backup singers. The titles were "Maybe I'm Right," "I Love My Baby," "Little Richard's Boogie," and "Directly From My Heart To You." Otis gave them a real sheen, buffing what were trite lyrics with shimmering orchestration. "Maybe," a sensuous ballad that either Esther or Etta could have sung, lifted Richard's voice in range and intensity, at times punctuating lines with a slight sigh of relief and a gushing *ooooh*. "Directly" was a blues stroll with a funky piano line and electric guitar break. "I Love My Baby" and "Little Richard's Boogie" were both dance shakers that prefigured later Little Richard work, taken up a notch by Otis's deft work on the vibes and the shouts of the band.

Yet before the sides could be released, Richard, nursing his wounds and pride after being decked by Robey, had split and went home to Macon for comfort, without a word to the Tempo Toppers or Robey, ruining plans to tour in support of the records. And apparently in spite, a frothing Robey, no matter the cost and trouble of putting the session together, nixed putting out any more Little Richard records, at least until Little Richard's massive success led him to belatedly release the remaining four sides credited to Little Richard with the Johnny Otis Orchestra. (They would not appear on an album until 2007, long after Robey was gone and his labels and song catalog sold and passed around from ABC to MCA. Rumors are that other Otis-produced Little Richard tracks exist as well. Richard would also rerecord "Directly" in the style of James Brown for Modern Records in 1966.)

The Tempo Toppers, left high and dry even before the Otis sessions, straggled back to Nashville, their sole brush with fame their brief shared role with an almost famous Little Richard, who for his part felt no guilt about ditching them. Rather, he felt an uplifting pride walking on the thuggish Don Robey, later saying, "I refused to let him control me. If I can't have freedom, I can't be happy. Contracts don't mean nothing to me if I can't be relaxed. A contract is only your word. Paper don't mean nothing to me." Robey, meanwhile, hardly batted an eye losing Richard. His sphere of influence would grow wider in the gospel blues niche, with Junior Parker and Bobby "Blue" Bland, enabling him to sell his labels to ABC for a bundle in 1973, two years before his death. Yet, in hindsight, he could blame only himself for losing out on a potential gold mine and a deeper root in history—that is, if he could have kept Little Richard and brought the best out of him. That, of course, was an open question, whether *anyone* could do that.

As it was, Richard's goals still seemed to be a contradiction: alloying the secular and the ecumenical, being bold and daring while conventionally spiritual, applying centuries-old canons to new abstractions of individualism and raw hedonism, even gender-twisting. Who, in a country clinging to age-old cultural norms—and in a business governed by exploitative white businessmen and black businessmen acting like exploitative white businessmen—would dare take a chance on him, knowing he would not be easy to stick in a safe corner of the music ring or keep mum about being stiffed?

The answer, as it happened, was waiting on the horizon, just down the road, in the hands of fate and in Little Richard's golden throat.

three

RIGHT RHYTHMIC
ROCK AND ROLL MUSIC

Little Richard and the Upsetters got this tremendous name. Fats
Domino would come to the Manhattan Club, in Macon, and I would go
out to see him. He was a star then, but he was playing the blues.
Chuck Berry was a star, too. But they were blues singers. They were
all afraid of me, 'cos they had heard people talking about me, saying,
'Have you been to Macon? Have you seen this guy Little Richard?
Y'know, he's terrible. Have you heard him play the piano?' My name
was getting all over the place. I was really out there with the people.

—LITTLE RICHARD

Contrary to popular opinion, Little Richard did not invent
rock and roll, a term that itself was not adopted as a discrete
idiom of music until the mid-1950s. Although it had been used
otherwise, including in Negro spirituals with a religious connotation,

the phrase was most commonly heard among the jazz crowd as a euphemism for sex or dancing, as in a 1935 ditty, "Get Rhythm in Your Feet," which had the line "If Satan starts to hound you, commence to rock and roll" and in ensuing years in songs by the likes of Ella Fitzgerald, the Andrews Sisters, Bing Crosby, country singer Buddy Jones—and, as Richard Penniman surely knew, Sister Rosetta Tharpe's shorthand usage of it in her song "Rock Me." And while it's unlikely he read *Billboard*, Richard would have completely agreed with a review in the showbiz trade paper of a version of "Caldonia" describing the song as "right rhythmic rock and roll music."

The carnal meanings of the term were not in doubt, though it was generic sounding enough to be "acceptable," a reality that continued when Alan Freed in 1951 began applying "rock and roll" to the new race music he played on the air in Cleveland, an important entry into the lives of white teenagers in the breadbasket of America. By then, given that rock was a spin-off of long-established blues and jazz, there is a great debate about which of those seminal soundings can be anointed as the first rock and roll record. The consensus is that it was Ike Turner's doing, not for his gritty blues songs with the then-Anna Mae Bullock (soon recast as Tina Turner) but a tune he composed for his band the Rhythm Kings, "Rocket 88," recorded in Sam Phillips's Sun Studio in Memphis in 1951 and released under the name of his sax player Jackie Brenston, who sang lead.

At the least, the song was the first of the era to center on a souped-up hot rod. And Little Richard would testify that its uninhibited, bass-driven boogie-shuffle beat, honking sax, fuzzy guitar (caused by a broken amp), and machine-gunning piano triplets—played by Turner—formed a template that had a dramatic influence on young musicians like him, especially the turning of a keyboard into a high-pitched engine—and not incidentally, the rapid pulse of a lusting libido. Every riff he would play, Richard said, was a variation of Turner's piano intro, which he reproduced note for note several times, such as his own intro on "Good Golly, Miss Molly" and throughout "Lucille."

In 1954, when Little Richard was still unheard in most of the country, rock was advancing on several geographic fronts, each defined by an indigenous sound derived from its blues roots. The most commercial was, typically, the Broadway-based Tin Pan Alley system of producers, composers, and favored singers, which spawned Bill Haley's rockabilly-flavored rock. Other Broadway gems came from Ahmet Ertegun's Atlantic Records, which stamped the new R&B with the tony harmonies of the original Drifters fronted by the buttery vocals of Clyde McPhatter, and the original "Shake, Rattle and Roll" with Big Joe Turner. And, uptown, at the small Rama label owned by George Goldner, whose roster of Harlem street corner soul included the Crows' "Gee" in 1953, its uninhibited lyrical riffing, high harmonies, and electric blues guitar solo were a true launching pad for rock.

In the breadbasket—in Chicago, Detroit, and Cleveland—the eventual destinations of so many of the old delta blues men who had emigrated northward, electric guitar masters like Muddy Waters, John Lee Hooker, Howlin' Wolf, and Lightnin' Hopkins were getting belated recognition. The hot label out of the Windy City, Chess Records, which had many of the hoary blues men, moved into rock—and it was Chess that licensed and released "Rocket 88" and in '54 signed an unknown singer/guitar man from St. Louis named Chuck Berry.

The Southern rock landscape was divided between the integrated black and hillbilly rockers under Sam Phillips's view in Memphis. That same year of 1954, Elvis made his first two records, his covers of Arthur Crudup's "That's Alright" and Roy Brown's "Good Rocking Tonight." Down in New Orleans, Fats Domino's first hit, "The Fat Man" in 1949, a variation of Willie Hall's "Junker Blues," was a palate of Creole, jazz scatting, rolling piano triplets, and a metronome back beat that also qualifies for consideration as the first—or at least oldest—rock and roll record, selling over a million copies on the blues-based Imperial label. And out on the coast, where Johnny Otis held sway, blues-bred acts mined by Federal Records included the Penguins' seminal doo-wop hit "Earth Angel" and the butter smooth group harmony of the Platters, both acts' material written and produced by Buck Ram, a white Jewish blues devotee who demanded that the giant Mercury label put his acts on its main roster, not on a "race record" sub-label, an important step forward for black performers.

This, then, was the lay of the land as mid-decade approached, its soundtrack a heavily echoed beat framed by booming bass bottoms—which, before electric bass, came pouring out of massive upright basses with linguine-thick strings—and amplified electric guitars at the top. It was sonic gumbo, far from technically perfect, yet the imperfections were precisely what gave this new/old sound its thump, its sweaty realness, the pure exhilaration of feeling good, and feeling horny—rock and roll's fundamental birthright. The most daring songs were the least concerned with good taste. Witness Hank Ballard's "Work with Me, Annie" and Billy Ward and His Dominoes' "Sixty Minute Man." What's more, the early '50s rockers knew how to get attention; they dressed to the nines in roomy, sharp houndstooth suits and two-tone shoes, another carryover from the R&B heyday. Indeed, the look, the sound, the milieu of rock were in place, grabbing for a chance to burgeon. In '53, RCA, which had been so clueless about the new sound, saw one of its old country releases, "Crying in the Chapel," covered by the

Orioles, who made it a major early crossover rock hit (later covered by Little Richard).

A pure rock song still had not made it high on the pop chart. The top-selling songs of 1953 included "Vaya Con Dios," and "(How Much Is) That Doggie in the Window?" In 1954, though, cracks began to open. Sandwiched between "Little Things Mean a Lot" and Doris Day's "Secret Love" in the top three songs of the year was the Crew-Cuts' "Sh-Boom (Life Could Be a Dream)," a vanilla cover of the original race record by the Chords—which itself rang in at number 26. Number 19 was "Earth Angel." Number 20 Bill Haley's "Shake, Rattle and Roll." Things were happening, in small, growing doses. What did remain as a hurdle was the emergence of an avatar who could blast it out in its purest form so clearly and honestly to teenagers that it would become close to a religion.

AS ALL THIS commotion was happening, however, Richard Penniman was again back at the Greyhound terminal, washing dishes, watching people, writing songs in the kitchen, now older and a bit more wizened but a contradiction to those who knew him. He was, technically, a two-time failure as a recording act but could fill the house at will out on the chitlin' circuit, where Clint Brantley kept booking his regular tours. To support him, at Brantley's urging he put together a steady traveling band, hiring an outfit backing the R&B duo Shirley and Lee during a stop in Nashville. The unit consisted of sax men Wilbert "Lee Diamond" Smith (who later cowrote Aaron Neville's "Tell It Like It Is") and Clifford "Gene" Burks, Nat "Buster" Daniel on electric guitar, and drummer Charles Connor.

"Richard talked to us about going back to Georgia with him," Connor remembered. "See, Richard didn't have a band. He had a guitarist from Memphis, Thomas Hartwell. He was Richard's music director, because he was playing with house bands. He was the only one that was traveling with Richard at that time. He was the one that came and told us that Richard wanted to see us and talk to us. I told Richard, 'Yeah, man, but I don't have no drums. I have to get my drums out of the pawn shop.' 'Cause we were down and out, man. We hadn't had a decent meal in three weeks, I had big holes in my shoes. And I said to him, 'Could you feed us, please?' And Richard did. Then he got my drums out of the pawn shop, paid my back hotel rent. That's how much he wanted us."

Connor, who was only 18 at the time, said, "I'd seen Richard at a club called the Club Tijuana in New Orleans, he was playing with the Temple [*sic*] Toppers. I knew that guy had a lot of talent. My mother knew of him, too. When I told her about going to Macon, she said, 'Little Richard, that's that boy who looks like a girl with all that long hair?' See, Richard already had a reputation, but he wanted a lot more. And he knew what he wanted us to do. We used to rehearse in Richard's house in his front room. And he had like 50 people outside listening.

"After the first week we were there, Richard said to me, 'Come with me, we're going to go to the train station on Fifth Street. We're going to follow this train about a mile or a mile-and-a-half.' And we watched this train pull off from the train station. And the train was pulling off. So the train went, 'ch-ch-ch-ch, ch-ch-ch-ch, ch-ch-ch-ch, ch-ch-ch-ch.' And as the train picked up, it went [faster], 'ch-ch-ch-ch-ch-ch-ch.' He said, 'Charles, that's the kind of beat. I don't know the values of the notes, but that's the kind of beat I want you to play behind me when we play.' I said, 'Well, you want eighth notes.' Those eighth notes had a lot of energy, man."

Richard filled out the band when they got to Macon, adding another sax man, Grady Gaines, and, critically, Olsie "Bassy"

Robinson on upright bass, giving the sound a thumping bottom. They were a tight, versatile band, able to keep up with Richard's mercurial changes of mood, tempo, and idiom, and would remain in his employ throughout his run at the top, the eclat of the Upsetters nearly as famous as Richard himself. They, too, wore makeup and matching garb, loving the latter, hating the former but accepting it as a necessary concession to the lucrative notoriety of the act. There was also a practical reason for it.

Richard called them the Upsetters, said Connor, because "We were supposed to go and upset every town we played in. Every town we were playing. And Richard would tell the saxophone player—he would tell all the musicians except me; I was sitting down behind the drums—'If another band jumps off the stage, I want you to jump off the top of the roof of the house!' He wanted you to outdo every other band . . . We'd wear loud clothes because we had to dress up like gay guys. We had to dress like gay guys in order to play the white clubs, so we wouldn't [seem to] be a threat to the white girls, so the white audience wouldn't see all those colored boys digging 'em."

On an artistic level, the Upsetters formed Richard's defining sound, always best heard on stage, epoxying all the threads of race music into a screaming, undulating effect, his explosiveness stoked by the accompanying blast of the band. In the clubs, audiences knew his obscure songs, singing them with him. Those packed houses netted he and the band fifteen dollars for each show, sometimes a hundred a week, and Richard was adamant that they all make the same as he. Whenever an established act would play in Macon, a Fats Domino or a still-climbing Chuck Berry, Richard recalled condescendingly that those "blues singers" would be in *his* shadow, in cold fear of not measuring up to him.

Yet, when he came off the road, there he was again at the bus station, a metaphor of his uncertainty about where he was headed.

When no record companies called on him, it occurred to him that Don Robey was blackballing him. He thought it might even be God's will, to redirect him to the ministry. But, for Little Richard, God worked in mysterious ways. Just when he could have headed for the pulpit, another door opened that kept him hopeful about music. It happened in early 1955, when Lloyd Price came to Macon for a show at the City Auditorium. Price was a very hot property, along with Fats Domino an early breakout from the New Orleans hub. His first record, "Lawdy Miss Clawdy," went to number one on the R&B chart in 1952 and sold over a million copies for the L.A.-based Specialty label. Though his ensuing releases were less successful, "Clawdy" built a large following for him and the signature sound first unveiled by Fats (who played piano on the record) and the studio musicians who gave it a distinctive shuffling, rumbling beat. One of many, Richard was so taken by the sound that he directed the Upsetters to play in the same manner.

Richard made it his business to be at the Auditorium when Price played, and he wangled his way through security to get an audience with him. Like most who played the circuit, Price knew of Little Richard, and was such a fan of his work that he urged Richard to make a demo on a reel-to-reel tape machine and send it to Specialty's president, Art Rupe. Lloyd gave him the company's Sunset Boulevard address and said he'd put in a good word for him. Within days, Richard gathered up some songs he'd written, and went into the studio at Hamp Swain's station, WBML. Only two of which, "Wonderin'" and "She's My Star," would have his piano as background; two others, "Directly From My Heart To You" and "I'm Just a Lonely Guy," were sung a cappella, with Richard making a direct pitch to Rupe to sign him on the latter. These were still not the kind of songs he longed to record, but he kept himself to gospel blues so as not to scare Specialty off. After the session, he took the reel-to-reel tape, carefully stuck it into an embossed envelope and mailed it off.

And then he waited . . . and waited.

SPECIALTY HAD PLENTY of more pressing business. The company, founded by Rupe in 1945, had assembled an impressive roster of blues and early rock and roll acts, tilling in particular the New Orleans crop. Along with Price, the company was given a huge boost by Eddie "Guitar Slim" Jones, who in 1953 recorded the important blues/gospel hit "The Things I Used to Do," his intricate, fuzzy electric guitar licks and plaintive vocal produced by a young piano player, R.C. Robinson, soon—when signed by Atlantic—to go by the name Ray Charles. The song went to number one and stayed on the R&B chart for 42 weeks, gaining crossover appeal in the white market (and was later covered by both James Brown and Jimi Hendrix). Rupe had also signed the gospel group the Soul Stirrers, whose lead singer was a honey-smooth tenor named Sam Cooke, a man who was mobbed by young girls on stage as he oozed sexuality while singing gospel. This stable leaped into stiff competition with L.A.'s main race record labels, Imperial, Federal, and Modern, the latter the home base at the time for John Lee Hooker and Etta James.

All of which meant nothing to Little Richard, who expected the company to stop dead and hear out his demo tape. Caught in limbo and not getting any younger, he would place calls to Rupe, demand to be put through to him, and when he was, demand to know, "When you going to record me?" Finally, after eight long months, if only to dispense with the nuisance, Rupe and his top A&R man, Robert "Bumps" Blackwell, had to search for the tape under a pile of others. Finding it, they played it, and despite the recording's poor quality, Blackwell—a former jazz bandleader who had first employed a young Ray Charles and Quincy Jones, and had produced "Lawdy Miss Clawdy"—recalled later that "the voice was unmistakably star material," and that Little Richard "had something to say and could say it better than anyone I could think of." As prescient as Bumps was, he didn't know the half of it.

Blackwell recommended that Rupe sign Richard, sight unseen. He said Rupe was not nearly as eager to do it but went along. (Rupe told the opposite story: that Bumps "didn't think much of" what he heard but Art said, "Let's sign him—he sounds like B.B. King!") But before a contract could be sent to Clint Brantley for Richard to sign, Rupe found out that Little Richard was still under contract to Peacock. What's more, Don Robey was still so incensed at the man who had walked out on him, he refused to let Richard out before he could exact more revenge—dunning him six hundred dollars. Rupe paid it for him.

Rupe was convinced that he had lucked into a real find. After talking with Richard by phone, and hearing that Richard was a big fan of Fats Domino's sound, Rupe scheduled a recording session on September 13 in New Orleans at what was the cosmic center of gravity for blues/rock: the J&M Recording Studio on Rampart Street, located in the back of a furniture store. But even at that point, Rupe had already learned that Richard Penniman, for all his talent, could be a royal pain. While awaiting word from Rupe about the demo tape, Richard had gotten himself arrested by Macon cops at a gas station during a very bizarre joyride with a woman soliciting men to have sex with her while he watched. Charged with lewd conduct, he was thrown in jail for a few days. It was the sort of activity that could get a star into big trouble. Though the incident would be kept out of the papers, according to Richard it kept him out of Macon, at least for a while. "I couldn't go back there no more because of that. We just stayed on the road."

He did, however, stick around long enough to sign the Specialty contract and then head out with the Upsetters for New Orleans for his third stab at widespread success. Cocky as he was, he might have harbored the thought that he was about to change the flow of history, riding the destiny of right rhythmic rock and roll. If so, he was the only one who thought so.

TUTTI FRUTTI

His hair was processed a foot high over his head. His shirt was so loud it looked as though he had drunk raspberry juice, malt, and greens and then thrown up all over himself. Man, he was a freak.

—**ROBERT "BUMPS" BLACKWELL** on Little Richard in 1955

I am not conceited! It's just that, well, the Spirit of the Lord came to Richard Penniman and entered into him.   —**LITTLE RICHARD**

When Little Richard got to New Orleans, he ran into an immediate problem. Unbeknownst to him, Art Rupe and Bumps Blackwell had hired the same elite core of musicians that played on Fats Domino and Lloyd Price sessions at J&M Studios. This seemed a drunkard's dream, a gift from the heavens, to be able to record here, with the musicians that created sonic magic, and whose sound Richard himself had instructed his own band to imitate.

Richard, though, hemmed and hawed. He wanted his guys in the room, insisting only they knew how to back him. Bumps wouldn't hear of it and was incredulous that an unproven talent would make a fuss upon being provided all-star backup.

They went around and around on the matter, with Blackwell having to vouch for some of the industry's most famous side men (one of whom, Huey "Piano" Smith, would be a star himself, fronting his band the Clowns). They were, as Blackwell said, "the best in New Orleans," gathered to play behind a singer they had never heard of, and whom they sized up with scorn.

"They all thought I was crazy," Richard looked back. "Didn't know what to make of me. They thought I was a kook."

Richard finally relented, leaving the Upsetters with nothing to do while Blackwell arranged the charts for the eight sides Richard would record. Only then did Bumps meet the artist at the center of the session, whom Blackwell recalled as "this cat in this loud shirt, with hair waxed up six inches above his head" who was "talking wild, thinking up stuff just to be different. I could tell he was a mega-personality." No matter his bona fides, or lack thereof, Richard came in calling the shots, or so he thought. One bone of contention was that he would not be permitted to play the piano. He demanded to play it on the first song he wanted to record, "She's My Star," which had been on his demo tape. Bumps allowed him the perk, and to pretty much self-produce the track, fitfully ordering around eye-rolling musicians who never caught a groove.

The vibe already strained, it would be no easier for Blackwell to get it right. He got a couple of songs done in a take or two, including an early cover of Little Willie Littlefield's "Kansas City," but the others were an ordeal. "Wonderin'," another song from the demo tape, took ten takes. "All Night Long" did, too. "Lonesome and

Blue" required five. With four songs done, Blackwell ended the session, not at all pleased.

Seeking to wash away their blues, Blackwell, Richard, and sax man Lee Allen wound up unwittingly breeding the new order of rock and roll when Richard ripped it up on the stage of the Dew Drop Inn, wailing out the raunchy song written in the Macon Greyhound station. "Tutti Frutti" was a revelation, its inscrutability clear from its opening scat—*Awop bop a loo mop a good goddamn.* And while Blackwell had cause to exclaim, "That's a hit!" he knew it could never fly with the original lyrics about a "good booty," encouraging one to "Grease it, make it easy."

To be sure, being banned from the radio by stations feeling the cold fear of the FCC threatening their licenses was a real factor, and not just for overt sexual banter but, in one impending case—the cracked 1956 classic "Transfusion" by Nervous Norvus—detailing the human toll, in blood, of a car wreck. But Blackwell had industry connections all over the place, it seemed. Needing a songwriter he could call in to tone down the song, he found one in New Orleans, a "little colored girl," as Blackwell described Dorothy LaBostrie, who was actually 27 and a habitué of the Rampart Street clubs. She had submitted several songs to Blackwell, and when he asked her to come over to the Dew Drop, she believed he wanted to record one. This was by design, as Bumps feared she wouldn't want to have any part of such a song. At the same time, Richard resented that anyone would rewrite his words.

Blackwell had to talk them both into it.

As it was, Richard was so embarrassed to recite the words in front of LaBostrie that he had to turn and face the wall. They then went back to the studio to resume the session, and as Richard cut four more tracks—a redo of his early song "Directly From My Heart to You," "Maybe I'm Right," "I'm Just a Lonely Guy," and "Baby"— LaBostrie worked on the cleaned-up "Tutti Frutti."

Finally, with time running out on the session, she was done. She had scrubbed the thornier phrases without altering the raison d'etre of the tune, allowing for liberal interpretations of verses built around, in Louis Jordan style, girls' names ("I got a girl named Sue / She knows just what to do" . . . . "I've got a gal named Daisy / She almost drives me crazy"). When Sue rocked to the east and rocked to the west, it meant only one thing. Nor did it disturb any of the intent that "good booty" was now the enigmatic "Aw-Rootie." Meanwhile, "A wop-bob. . ." remained undisturbed, though edited to *a-wop-bop-a-loo-mop-a-lop-bam-boom*, clearly the mating call of a new generation, no matter its derivation.

If the lyrics were catnip to future listeners, in the studio the most famous opening to a song in rock history gave the session its marching order. It was how he and the Upsetters had played "Tutti Frutti" on the road.

"'A-wop-bop-a-loo-bop' came from my drum sound, how I used my kick drum with the snare," said Charles Connor. "So instead of the drum he just sang how it sounded. That sort of kicked the whole thing into overdrive right from the start," unleashing a torrent of coherent yet wild rhythm. And, to Richard's surprise, the studio musicians got the groove just fine.

Because there hadn't been time to chart an arrangement, Blackwell recorded it as a stage performance, letting the musicians wing it, according to their instinct. And because it would all flow from Richard, Bumps had him on piano, gliding and banging up and down the keyboard with abandon. That "wild piano," Blackwell said, "was essential to the success of the song." He recalled putting a microphone between Richard and the piano and another *inside* the piano. Back in those prehistoric days of recording, with just two tracks on their machines, such simple techniques could create miraculous sonic effects; here, a larger, fuller, double-tracking effect was created, swelling the sound into a ball of rhythm driving the production. The musicians, finally in sync with the singer, blew the roof off, instinctively extending or truncating notes by the changes in Richard's voice, even his movements. Lee Allen, who got on the same wavelength backing Richard at the Dew Drop, fastened an itchy honking sax part, filling the top above the rumbling rhythm of Earl Palmer's snare drum and sinewy growl of Frank Fields's bass.

Richard, of course, knew precisely what he wanted to hear. Years later he told *Rolling Stone*, "I used to play piano for the church. You know that spiritual, 'Give Me that Old Time Religion,' most churches just say, [sings] 'Give me that old time religion' but I did, [sings] 'Give me that old time, talkin' 'bout religion,' you know I put that little thing in it, you know, I always did have that thing but I didn't know what to do with the thing I had. So the style has always been with me but I had never introduced it for the people to hear. Because I would hear Fats Domino, Chuck Berry, Ruth Brown, Faye Adams, the Clovers, the Drifters, Muddy Waters, Howlin' Wolf, John Lee Hooker, Elmore James, and I admired them, but I always had my little thing I wanted to let the world hear, you know."

That anything cohesive came out of those New Orleans 1955 sessions was a tribute to collective genius that lifted them high above the stone-age conditions of a then-typical recording studio. Richard recalled that "[t]he studio was about 15 by 10 feet, air coming from everywhere; in the wintertime we froze, if he was playing saxophone he was a froze saxophone player. And I would sit there, man, and play, and me and the band would get together and jam and pick out riffs, and I'd hum ideas to them, pick them out on the piano, and we never missed, because I always came out with something different."

Richard had his own new wrinkle on the piano at that "Tutti Frutti" session. Rather than his right hand playing the melodic chords and the left the bass notes, he played the melody with both, banging away on the highest notes, muscling up on the hypnotic rhythm. Two takes were done; the first was the one Bumps went with.

It was a take that would alter history.

THE SESSION ENDED with racing pulses, a far cry from the somnolent despair of the previous one, and the group dispersed, Richard and the cuckolded Upsetters heading back on the road. Meanwhile, when Blackwell returned to L.A. and played the new Little Richard songs, Art Rupe heard only two cuts as possible single releases: "Kansas City" and the uproarious "Tutti Frutti." Blackwell was sold on the latter and began the process of mixing the record in preparation for an October release. And Rupe was so convinced that he had a winner in Little Richard that he sent him an airplane ticket to come out to L.A. for a session at Radio Recorders Studio to record a second version of "Kansas City," which had been extensively reworked by Blackwell and Rupe to be bigger and more compelling, including hiring a chorale of female backup singers and adding a repeating hook of "Hey hey hey hey."

Richard complied, unaware that "Tutti Frutti" had already been chosen as his breakout. He took his first airplane ride and entered the City of Angels playing the part of Mr. Hollywood. As Bumps recalled, "he was so far out!" The clothes, the hair, the makeup. In full freak mode. Even in La-La-Land, he was a sight. And he had no trouble seeking out fellow freaks to spend time with. Bumps had to buy him a new, less demonstrative wardrobe just to walk comfortably down the street with him. But if anyone was ever comfortable with himself, it was Richard Penniman. And that ease was the trait that carried his music.

"He had that magic," Blackwell said, "that perception, which made him able to handle an audience." That was the magic that Rupe sensed in him, the one he wanted to stoke when he sent for Richard to redo the more biting version of "Kansas City" backed by Guitar Slim's band, which required eight meticulous takes, as well as rerecording "Wonderin'" and "Baby," plus "Miss Ann," "True Fine Mama," and the earliest takes of two others that he'd been performing on the road, "Slippin' and Slidin'" and "Long Tall Sally"—the last needing eight frustrating takes. Indeed, Blackwell was so dissatisfied in general with the recordings that he added three more sessions at different studios in L.A., hoping the acoustics would be better. Several of these tracks would be only of vocals or overdubs, done before Bumps stopped and went on to the next song. None of the tracks would ever be released.

And Richard was once more caught in limbo. He had heard songs of his on the radio before. They had become regional hits, only to fail to go anywhere on the national charts and soon be pushed aside. The latest release, in mid-October 1955, was "Tutti Frutti," labeled as Specialty 561, with the B-side "I'm Just a Lonely Guy," both under the name "Little Richard And His Band" and the writing credits "LaBostrie-Penniman." It was shipped to both black and white radio stations in the big markets to create a buzz with subsequent shipping to record stores. The first Richard heard it, he was back in Macon, up at night and listening to Nashville's WLAC. The 50,000-watt radio station had a standard mainstream format but, after dark, when other stations on its frequency went off the air, it sent R&B programs so far across the map that the station billed itself as "the nighttime station for half the nation."

For black listeners, it was a rhythmic pulse, the new sound of rock purveyed by disc jockeys like John "John R" Richbourg and Gene Nobles, whose show Richard was tuned to when Nobles pronounced, "This is the hottest record in the country. This guy Little Richard is taking the record market by storm," and rolled out "Tutti Frutti."

"I couldn't believe it," he remembered. "My old song a hit!"

Not just any old hit, either. The song hit the ground not so much running, but sprinting like Jesse Owens down the track. By late November, it hit the *Billboard* "Best Sellers in Stores" R&B chart, number twelve in its first week there; the next week, it was at number ten, ahead of the Robins' "Smokey Joe's Cafe" and the Turbans' "When You Dance." Just after the new year, it hit its peak, number two, kept from the top by the Platters' smash "The Great Pretender," and ahead of the El Dorados' "At My Front Door (Crazy Little Mama)." It was also among the top entries on the "Most Played in Juke Boxes" and "Most Played by Jockeys" charts, an indication that its reach extended to the now-coveted teen market, heard on the Top 40 stations. That was the cue for white singers to get in on the budding rock craze by requisitioning hot "race records" and making them even more palatable to the teenagers of the white market.

This trend could take some mighty strange turns. Another record, "I Hear You Knockin'," recorded at J&M Studios by Smiley Lewis for Imperial Records, made the R&B chart before "Tutti Frutti" and also went to number two. A variation of "Hound Dog," the song was covered in short order by, of all people, pert actress Gale Storm, star of the vanilla TV sitcom *My Little Margie* (one of the characters of which was a shuffling, Stepin Fetchit-type black elevator man). Despite what is obvious now, that this version was, as one critic has put it, "a ludicrous whitewashed cover of the plaintive ballad," it reached number two on the Hot 100 singles chart and went gold. By contrast, Lewis's record sold 100,000 copies, leading the song's writer, Dave Bartholomew, to say that Margie "killed" the original. (Fats Domino's 1961 cover also went gold, though Little Richard's own later version was not as successful.)

Richard's first experience being ripped off in this way came when the even more vanilla Pat Boone somehow became adept at parlaying the blackest songs to the whitest audience. Earlier in 1955, the crooner had covered Fats Domino's "Ain't That a Shame" (cowritten by Fats and Bartholomew), whereupon the strength and cleverness of the song was heard for the first time by many white ears. As a result, the record soared to the top of the pop chart, and even number fourteen on the R&B chart (and number seven in England, the first time a race record, albeit without being known as such, went top ten across the pond). Most bizarre is that black genius made Pat Boone a white star, and of course demanded that he play the same card. He did so with "At My Front Door" (number seven pop, twelve R&B) and then the Flamingos' gushy ballad "I'll Be Home," which had gone to number 5 on the R&B chart. As the B-side for the latter, Boone's record company, Dot, picked "Tutti Frutti."

No more bizarrely misaligned aural products exist in the history of mankind, yet the ersatz "Tutti Frutti," which ironically means "all colors" in Italian, caught the public fancy. After "I'll Be Home" went to number four on the pop chart and number one in England, its flip side went off on its own run, hitting number 12 on the pop chart. Naturally, this made for a real conundrum for Richard. He, like Smiley Lewis, felt violated. But, having cowritten the song, he—like Domino and Bartholomew with "Shame"—was enriched by it indirectly. Then, too, as with the earlier rip-offs, the song's exposure to the white market inevitably lifted the original into crossover territory, moving "Tutti Frutti" up to number twenty-one on the pop list, another crucial ten-pin in the evolution of rock and roll. Even so, Richard never got over the feeling of personal resentment (which, years thereafter, Pat Boone would sympathize with, freely admitting that his cover versions of great black soul men were indeed pallid, casting himself as an innocent instrument of the designs of the industry). Despite having broadened the idiom of rock, Richard said, he was still relegated to outsider status.

"I felt I was pushed into a rhythm and blues corner to keep out of the rockers' way, because that's where the money is," he said.

That bitter contradiction that his record was better than any in the white rock corner, and the sometimes-secret guilty pleasure of white teens, yet shunted aside for an inferior version had a simple predicate. "They needed a rock star to block me out of white homes because I was a hero to white kids," he went on. "The white kids would have Pat Boone up on the dresser and me in the drawer 'cause they liked my version better, but the families didn't want me because of the image I was projecting."

Even more baffling, and galling in retrospect, is that even Elvis Presley's far more convincing cover of "Tutti Frutti," which was included on his first album, was dwarfed in the public eye by Boone's anemic one. And it was such doses of reality, aided by conscious marketing decisions, that left many black rockers attempting to tailor their acts to keep from sounding *too* black. Take Chuck Berry, for example. As catchy and rockin' as were his first trove of songs—his debut, "Maybellene," released in the summer of '55, hit number one on the R&B chart and number five on the pop—he was a different cat than Richard, bred in the north, his songs an amalgam of the race records of Delta bluesmen like Muddy Waters and the tony mainstream soul pop of Nat King Cole. His vocals, he explained, were "calculated" as "harder and whiter," and that "it was my intention to hold both the black and white clientele by voicing different kinds of songs in their customary tongues." Atlantic

Records honcho Jerry Wexler once noted that while Berry and Little Richard "were targeted for teens, Berry was writing for white adolescents out of a country bag, and his diction is unalloyed white middle America."

To be accurate, that was also Richard's target audience. But their acceptance was on *his* terms, not theirs. Richard had no chameleon tendencies. He had one and only one native tongue, that of Deep South blues and gospel, which he applied to the big bang of rock and roll. That was his offer, take it or leave it. And America seemed to be taking it, and if for many teens it meant having to hide their race records from their parents, the older generation was being exposed to the new idiom on venues they had become welded to. For example, an important capstone came in November 1955 when Ed Sullivan, a race music buff, putting occasional black artists on his top-rated Sunday night variety show on CBS, devoted a twelve-minute block to R&B/rock stars Bo Diddley, LaVern Baker, the Five Keys, and Willis "Gator Tail" Jackson. Eight years after Jackie Robinson broke baseball's pernicious color line, the walls of pop music were crumbling down, and Little Richard was riding the bulldozer.

ART RUPE, WILLING to gamble on the timing of it all, had stumbled into a gold mine, mainly for himself. And that created trouble. The half-cent royalty return on sales was bad enough, but worse was that, as a condition for signing, Richard had to sell the publishing rights to his songs, rights that he didn't even know existed, grabbing the nominal fifty dollar meed for each handover. Rupe would then funnel the publishing royalties of Richard's hit songs to his own publishing company. Those royalties would have brought Richard a ton of green. In time, he would realize how much of a victim he was: "I got a half cent for every record sold," he would say, adding incredulously, "Whoever heard of cutting a penny in half?" He would also say, quite correctly, that he had signed "a very bad deal," one that was essentially no different than the deal that had caused the same kind of rift with Don Robey, only worse.

For his part, Rupe defended himself as a benefactor, one who allowed his artists their own space to grow. "I made plenty of money," he said. "My artists made plenty of money. I didn't share on their personal appearances. I gave them a very fair contract, particularly [to] an unknown [and] I was very scrupulous in paying the royalties, not only accurately but in a timely manner . . . unlike a lot of people in the industry." Richard would still make fair money (the writing royalties couldn't be denied him; they were determined by outside accountants at BMI or ASCAP), as would Dorothy LaBostrie.

With no earthly idea that "Tutti Frutti" would one day be hailed as "the sound of the birth of rock and roll," LaBostrie was tickled to death when *her* royalty checks rolled in. To her dying day in 2007, she was receiving checks for $50,000 twice or thrice a year. In later years, she bridled when Richard, amplifying on his claims that he never received due royalties on the song, insisted he had written the tune all by himself, not explaining why LaBostrie got on the credit line. To the contrary, she claimed, *she* alone deserved credit. "Little Richard," she said, "didn't write none of 'Tutti Frutti.'" Of course, that was sheer fiction. At the *very* least, Richard had touched off a craze and a brand new idiom simply with the ten-syllable locution of deep, profound gibberish that began the song, gibberish that the Library of Congress in 2010 would bestow immortality to, adding the song to its registry for its "unique vocalizing over the irresistible beat [that] announced a new era in music"; and which *Rolling Stone* codified as "the most inspired rock lyric ever recorded"—though "lyric" doesn't begin to explain what *a-wop-bop-a-loo-mop-a-lop-bam-boom* is.

Immortality, however, was not on Richard's mind in 1955. Although he would spend a good deal of his money on a series of lawsuits against Rupe and the subsequent powers that would enter after Rupe sold off his company, in real time he always had to focus on repeating the success of each record he made. That was the hard part, the real work. When he was out on the road, which was basically his home, and where the money was, he and the Upsetters were now pulling five figures a week, and Richard would be generous with them, that is, when he was happy. When he brooded, they had to ask, and ask again, for even basic expenses. Arguments and outright fights were many, though in the end all of the band members remained loyal to him and kept a good many of his secrets. In return, the Upsetters claimed a modicum of fame for themselves, which allowed them to be able to perform under their own imprimatur when Richard was busy or, later, too hungover or stoned to make a show. As Richard became more of a shining nova, they would still tour, able to get by fronting a singer to stand in for Richard.

One of the occasions when Richard left them on their own brought about a legendary twist of fate. It happened when Rupe again brought Richard out to L.A. after the new year of 1956 for a round of post-"Tutti Frutti" appearances and interviews with the trade papers. At the time, he and the Upsetters were about to do a series of gigs, but Richard had no contrition leaving Brantley and the band in the lurch. Clint stewed about it but dug up another singer to stand in for Richard. That singer was James Brown. A year younger than Richard, born in South Carolina, Brown had moved to Georgia, served a stretch in a juvenile correction facility, then turned to singing gospel and rhythm and blues with a band that, as he moved up, would become the Famous Flames.

Clearly influenced by Little Richard, though shorter, stocky, and nowhere near as pretty, his hair was also piled high atop his head. The difference was that James could dance. His performances were an eddy, as he twisted his feet and worked into a sweat-covered furor, falling to his knees and springing back up, his sandpaper voice digging deep into the soul. Bathed as he was in sweat, he had a shtick, even then, doubling over and melodramatically dropping to his knees, cradling the microphone in trembling hands. Where Richard sang of joy and balling, James was the sound of a cleaved heart.

Charles Connor laughed when he recalled Brown standing in for Richard. As markedly different as they looked and sounded, he said, "It was Little Richard's picture on the placards. And people would say, 'He don't look like Little Richard to me—but he sounds good!'" Richard himself was impressed by Brown; he'd told Brantley to sign James, after all. And the connection with Little Richard paid off for James in many ways, ways that he, well, *borrowed.* At another show, he heard the emcee introduce the headliner by saying, "Ladies and gentlemen—the hardest-working man in show business today—Little Richard!" Brown began having himself introduced that way, and it would stick. And according to Connor, who would also be in Brown's band later on, James's most famous shtick—someone draping a shawl over his shoulders whereupon he would limp away, then turn on a dime, throw off the shawl, and belt out the song—was also lifted.

"Richard did it first," Connor insisted. "He would fall on the floor and act like he's passing out. He had a roadie put the cape on him and then when he started sweating he'd throw it off, sometimes into the audience. James copied that, too."

Brown was the only human being who could have taken Little Richard's place on a stage and get away with it—not that Richard would ever pass up noting, apropos of nothing, that he had not only "discovered" James but had "got him out of jail." Still, when Richard returned from L.A., the two men became friendly, Richard's ear for dialect making him one of the few people who could understand Brown's fractured English. When they had lunch one day, they batted around ideas for a song James could make his first recording. Richard scribbled on a napkin, "Please, Please, Please," gleaning James's niche for emotional yearning. Brown took it from there, fleshing out sparse lyrics for a song with that title, a ballad in which he pleaded, "Don't go. . . I love you so." Brantley then called Hamp Swain, who, as Zenas Sears had done for Richard, arranged for a recording session for Brown and his Famous Flames at Swain's Macon, Georgia, radio station, WIBB, in the Professional Building on Mulberry Street.

The tape of that session, which also included another Brown ballad, "Try Me," would win Brown his first recording contract, with King Records. In March 1956 a version of "Please, Please, Please" rerecorded at the label's Cincinnati studio—with Brown and a collaborator named Johnny Terry credited as the writers—was released and raced to number six on the R&B chart, selling a million copies. ("Try Me" would go to number one on the R&B in 1958, kicking off Brown's long, winding, quaking road in soul and funk.)

As Brown began to rise, he was so wedded to Charles Connor's drum licks that he tried to pry him away from Richard. "James wanted me to go on the road with him, too. I said, 'Well, James, I'm going to tell you, I don't mind, but I can't disappoint Richard because Richard was the one that helped me when I didn't have nothing, paying my hotel rent, and he bought me shoes, and he fed me and everything.' So that would have been a guilt trip, that's why I didn't go with James Brown. He wanted to take me on the road, too. But I remained with Richard."

Richard, meanwhile, was hardly gathering any moss. He was constantly in demand, constantly heard on the radio, his "old" record flying off the shelves. Yet, as he looked at where he was going after "Tutti Frutti," the world wasn't enough. He wanted more. He wanted it all. The sun and the moon and the stars. But he could only get there if he were able somehow to keep lifting himself higher and higher, even if every step upward was in conflict with himself.

WHOLE LOT OF
RHYTHM GOIN' 'ROUND

I don't know what all the fussin' is about. Everybody knows people
make love. They had to make love for you and I to be sittin' here today.
Old people try to make sex sound so bad and all but it's beautiful.
Wonderful thing, thank God for sex!   **—LITTLE RICHARD**

He could put the fear of God in you while singing about getting laid.
                                        —OTIS WILLIAMS, the Temptations

Specialty Records president Art Rupe would keep Little Richard very busy in the studio. With "Tutti Frutti" still selling
well, Rupe and Blackwell scheduled a new session on February 10,
1956, at J&M Studios in New Orleans, to cut new material that
would produce the pivotal follow-up to "Frutti," which Rupe determined had to be better than "Kansas City." That song, Rupe would

have Richard rework again under the title "Hey-Hey-Hey-Hey! Goin' Back to Birmingham" (with the writing credit solely Richard's, Leiber and Stoller being stiffed). Yet Rupe was never satisfied with it, and the first of the three versions, once regarded as an ace card, would sit on the shelf until it was put on the 1970 Little Richard compilation album *Well Again.*

Richard, too, knew he would have to go beyond even the dizzying scope of "Tutti Frutti." As much of a rock-and-roll pivot point as it was, it had not fully met *his* expectations. Playing the song as the biggest payoff punch of his act, he ordered the Upsetters to give no attention to the record that had stormed up the charts. As Chuck Connor recalled, "Richard said to us, 'I want "Tutti Frutti" to have a little more energy to it. I don't want that single back-beat like when Earl Palmer played it in the studio.' He made me change it so it was more heavy on the bass drum." To Connor, the beat Richard wanted was something unheard of then, something so unearthly that, two decades later, when music was being formulated by frantic, bass-thick arrangements, he would look back on "Tutti Frutti" as the very model of "the disco beat." But what it really was, was Little Richard unchained.

As Connor saw it, there was no contest between the studio sound, which he thought was processed and pallid, and the hellzapoppin' of the live performances. "The same guys that recorded a lot of songs behind Richard, they recorded behind Fats Domino, they recorded behind Shirley and Lee, behind Ernie K-Doe, behind Smiley Lewis, and all those guys. But they couldn't have gone on the road with Richard, because they were too old. I mean, we were young good-looking guys. Earl Palmer and Frank Fields and all those guys, those guys were about thirty-two, thirty-three years old. But the tunes that we wasn't on with Richard, we would do the tunes and Richard would say, 'Go tell the musicians in the studio how we did it,' and how he wanted it done."

Richard's geyser of popularity and stardom had numerous implications, one of which was that Clint Brantley was given the gate. This happened once Richard knew he had become too big for Macon. For a brief but heady time, Clint found himself in charge of the two hottest race music stars in the galaxy, Richard and James Brown. However, he may have guessed he was on borrowed time with Richard, who had the same resentments with him that he had with Don Robey and Art Rupe, the issue of course being the same with them all: money—or lack thereof.

Richard suspected Clint was shaving way too much off the top. Having worked his way up the ladder basically on his own and now a part of the Hollywood in-crowd, Richard considered Brantley to be not just a small-timer but a small-timer and a crook. Now, with a massive hit and a tight bond with Bumps Blackwell, Richard was easily won over when Bumps made a move into management. Bumps had power, connections, and soon after Richard fired Brantley, who would feel the sting for the rest of his days. In later years, while not addressing Richard's aspersions that he ripped him off, Clint claimed he had gone to the mat for Richard, without appreciation.

"Richard, he was gonna fuck with you," he said. "That's the difference between him and James Brown. I told James one time that I needed $2,000; I owed it to a cracker. And a few days later that $2,000 was here. James did everything he could for me. I didn't have to ask him to do it, he did it. Richard didn't ever do a damned thing. All I got out of Richard, I took it."

Although his last line could be construed as proof that Richard was right about him, Brantley maintained that living with Little Richard, his quirks, his craziness, his moods, was sheer hell. Added to those of James Brown, he must have felt he needed to wear combat gear, especially when Brown got into a Wild West shootout after a Macon concert with soul singer Joe Tex that left seven wounded (no charges were filed after Brown paid the victims off). At least Richard avoided such incidents—though he, too, carried guns on the road for protection. But in a sense Clint caught a break, inasmuch as Richard had not even begun to scratch the surface of his later descent into drugs and immoral escapades that would have kept Brantley busy tearing his hair out. Still, it was a double blow to the gut when first Richard, then James, severed their ties with him, effectively ending his reign as a local power broker just as race music was burgeoning into mainstream tastes. The timing was truly terrible. Brown's "Try Me" was the first of seventeen number one R&B hits. And Richard was about to embark on a three-year whirlwind when nothing seemed beyond his reach.

Not needing to wait for the full force of his success, and far beyond the need to stay in Macon, Richard pulled up stakes and moved all the way across the country, to the smoggy environs of Los Angeles, buying a big, $25,000 house on Virginia Road in the Sugar Hill section of the West Los Angeles city of Riverside. It was a formerly white neighborhood where among the few minority residents was the former heavyweight champ Joe Louis, who Richard claimed had grown up like him in Macon though Louis was raised in Alabama. Richard employed his brother Marquette as a valet on his road travels. Then, in 1956, he moved Leva Mae and Enotris Johnson, along with Richard's brothers and sisters, into the house, too. To be able to afford the lavish digs, Richard had asked Rupe for a loan of the twenty-five grand, not understanding that it would be deducted from his incipient royalties, as were studio and musician fees.

Looking back, he regarded this time of his life as the happiest he ever had. The best part was the look on Leva Mae's face when she saw her new home. "She had never seen black people living in this type of house," he said, adding that "until they saw the house and my 1956 gold Fleetwood Cadillac in the garage they never realized what a big hit record really meant. And I didn't either."

What it meant in the short run was that the next time royalties were to be paid, rather than being owed, *he* owed the company. As time went on, he wouldn't record and tour simply because of the demand for his music. He *had* to, just to get by. Which at this point of his life meant living the Hollywood celebrity lifestyle.

As it turned out, fame itself was as much a rush as the money. It was an aphrodisiac that fed unabridged partying with manifestations of sexuality—gay, straight, whatever. Increasingly, sex was the very context of his life, off the stage and on. In 1956, during a show at the Royal Theatre in Baltimore, some of the females in the crowd slipped off their panties and threw them on stage, which according to Richard was "the first time" this rock ritual emerged. That show had to be stopped a few times when crazed crowds got too rowdy, fans even leaping from the balcony and trying to lay hands on him.

Charles Connor had an unobstructed view of all this mayhem from where he sat behind his drums. He remembered the time in Amarillo, Texas, when redneck cops, trying to preempt such scenes, would warn Richard not to act out too much, at the risk of arrest. "A lot of places we played down South, like Amarillo, they locked Richard up [to keep him] from shaking [his] hips on the bandstand. They'd stop the concert and throw him in jail. Richard's road manager would have to pay a fine, $150, $200. And then they'd say, 'You better not come back here shaking your hips like that, boy.' I'll never forget that night, because when they let him out they said, 'There's another guy coming here. He shakes his hips and everything like you. His name is Elvis Presley. If you see Elvis Presley, tell him he'd better not bring his redneck behind here shaking and acting the fool on the stage like colored people. 'Cause we're gonna lock him up, too!' Because Elvis was shakin' his behind on Ed

Sullivan, but in Amarillo all it meant was that a white man acting like a black man, and they couldn't have that."

SUCH INTERDICTIONS WERE rare; indeed, Richard may have been the least offensive "dangerous" rocker around. No matter the risk of becoming famous while black, he would usually skate right over it. His star shined so bright that some Jim Crow laws seemed not to apply to him.

Even while performing in the South, Richard rarely would be barred from staying at whatever lodging he chose. Those ropes separating the races would come down, if only for him. Existing in this rarefied air for a black man, he cut himself all the slack he needed to practice societal deviations. Richard never had any compunction implying he was gay, or as he later clarified his sexual thirsts, "omnisexual." To be sure, he played it as safe as he would accept in his songs, never outwardly singing anything that could be construed as gay; instead, themes were all generic scenarios of romance, lust, and conquest. And Richard himself was unsure from day to day what he wanted in particular, men or women. It seemed to be purely spur-of-the-moment.

Much of the time he seemed to be content pleasing himself while watching others go at it, which predicated a natural joke, later to be told by Woody Allen, that masturbation was sex with someone he loved. In his authorized biography, Richard boasted with real pride, "I used to do it six or seven times a day. In fact, everybody used to tell me that I should get a trophy for it, I did it so much. I got to be a professional jack-offer. I would do it just to be doing something." He told of hotel-room parties with the Upsetters when he was mainly a spectator to such episodes, like the time they had carnal knowledge of a woman while her husband was trying to find her, banging on doors, then sneaking her out of the room on the fire escape. When they played shows in St. Louis, a not-yet-of-age Etta James, who sang as an opening act, later came to the hotel and knocked on their door. Richard yelled to the others, "Don't open the door, she's a minor!" As she recalled, "Then one day, I climbed up and looked through the transom—and the things I *saw*!"

ART RUPE AND Bumps Blackwell had consciously wanted the follow-up to "Frutti" to be one that Pat Boone or any other white singer couldn't possibly cover. As Bumps recalled, it had to be so uptempo and "the lyrics going so fast that Boone wouldn't be able to get his mouth together to do it!" They had settled on several in that mode, including another go at "Miss Ann" and the first go at "Hey-Hey-Hey-Hey," "Rip It Up," and "Ready Teddy." All these were prime work, proof that as collaborators Richard and Blackwell were in a cosmic groove, knowing how to get the best last ounce of juice from the rising star. Any could have been released next, and all would have their day when they were. But it was another song that came to the fore. This was "Long Tall Sally," the first try at which had come at the L.A. sessions the previous November, the rough cut of which had been cataloged under the title "The Thing" (and can be heard on bootleg copies of the tape).

The genesis of this song is an enigma. As Blackwell told it in Richard's authorized biography, a disk jockey he identified as Honey Chile told him a little girl from Mississippi had written three lines of a song she wanted Richard to record so she could pay the hospital bills for a sick aunt. None of this, however, can be backed up. No DJ with that handle exists in history (one named "Honey Boy

Hardy" did host a gospel radio show in New Orleans at the time), and while Blackwell said the girl's name was "Enotiris Johnson," the name of Richard's adoptive father was *Enotris* Johnson, who would be listed as the song's cowriter with Richard and Bumps. Then, too, in 1970 Richard told his story about the old lady "built for speed" in his old neighborhood and her old man "Uncle John." Most likely, Richard had inserted Johnson into the credits in order to earn some money for his mother—as he would do by crediting Johnson on two other songs, "Miss Ann" and "Jenny, Jenny."

With a session set for February 7, 1956, in New Orleans, "Long Tall Sally" would involve the same musicians that made "Tutti Frutti" a hit, but in this and all ensuing sessions Richard would play the piano on all tracks, as not even the brilliant Huey Smith could get the double-right-hand chords and shuffling melody quite as well or as slick as Richard could. Unlike "Frutti," no lines needed to be sanitized; gentle sexual allusions to "bald-head Sally," Uncle John seeing Aunt Mary and ducking back in the alley, and the proud boast of "Havin' me some fun tonight" were all part of another explosion of sound created by the band's relentless shuffle beat, Lee Allen's brain-blasting sax, and Richard's staccato piano triplets. Other gems came from this session, too, including the second versions of "Rip It Up" and "Hey-Hey-Hey-Hey (Goin' Back to Birmingham)." There were also four takes of an early version of "Ready Teddy," three of an early try at "Heeby-Jeebies," and four of "The Most I Can Offer," four of "Oh Why?," plus seven of "Slippin' and Slidin' (Peepin' and Hidin')."

"Rip It Up" marked the brief but significant entry of another writer into the Little Richard circle, John Marascalco. A 25-year-old Mississippian, he had written "Rip It Up" and "Ready Teddy" specifically for Richard and drove cross-country to L.A. to pitch them to Bumps Blackwell, who agreed they were Richard material, with some alterations, lifting a cowriter's credit for himself on both songs. Unsatisfied with the first attempt at recording "Rip It Up," the second time was the charm—but only after Richard had taken a crack at it in fourteen exhausting takes.

The template of all Little Richard songs still sounded fresh, and the song began with the immortal rock and roll meme: "Well, it's Saturday night and I just got paid / Fool about my money, don't try to save," followed by repeated hooks about how he would rock it up, shake it up, ball it up, "and ball tonight"—the "balling" part giving Blackwell some pause, until Richard convinced him that the phrase was generic enough, not only slang for sex but for simply dancing, which naturally applied to the Little Richard milieu, as did the lines about picking up a date "in my 88." Bumps also left in the line "Shag on down by the union hall," the British slang for sex not yet in common usage. It all fit cheekily within the splashes of rhythm and spiky dance beat.

As for "Slippin and Slidin'," it was a cover of a song first recorded by Gene Phillips in 1950, covered a year later by Calvin Bozes, again by Al Collins with the title "I Got the Blues for You," and yet again by Eddie Bo. Richard made his own changes, retitling it "Slippin' and Slidin' (Peepin' and Hidin')," suggestive of Big Mama Thornton's "Hound Dog" with hep-cat phrasing such as "Done got hip to your jive," his punch line the vow "Won't be your fool no more!" This, too, was recorded within the now typical Little Richard rhythm casserole, giving Bumps three hit-level sides. He released two of them on the same disc—"Long Tall Sally" and "Slippin' and Slidin' (Peepin' and Hidin')" on the flip. Within a month, "Sally" had sold half a million and zoomed to number one on the R&B list, thirteen on the pop chart, to remain on the former for sixteen weeks. (According to another of those *Rolling Stone* lists, it is ranked as the fifty-fifth Greatest Song of All Time.)

And, as it happened, Blackwell was wrong. Pat Boone *did* cover "Long Tall Sally," originally as the B-side of a song called "Just As Long As I'm With You"—with Dot Records oddly listing only "Johnson" as the songwriter, stiffing Richard completely. And even though Boone was unable to replicate Richard's itchy cadences he still took the tune to number eight on the pop chart, eighteen on the R&B. Later, Richard would have to sue to collect back royalties as a writer on the song, but by then he was on a higher plane, helping turn the tide for all black artists. His classic version of "Sally" sold more than Boone's soon forgotten rip-off, prompting the latter to switch from terrible "race record" covers to soothing, soft white pop, his real niche, becoming one of the biggest-selling artists in the world in rock's teen-idol era.

Far better white imitators of race music, Elvis and Eddie Cochran, also recorded covers of "Sally," though Elvis's take only appeared on his 1956 *Elvis* album and Cochran's not at all until, posthumously, in 1962. In England, meanwhile, where Richard's original got to number three, it solidified the young Paul McCartney's ambition and when he joined John Lennon's first band the Quarrymen, the song became a part of their act. And Richard's step-by-step annexation of rock's emerging turf continued when "Slippin' and Slidin' (Peepin' and Hidin')" broke on a run of its own, to chart as number two for R&B and thirty-three for pop, spawning covers that included one by Buddy Holly. Suddenly—and it seemed to happen in the blink of a mascaraed eye—Little Richard had a stage act packed with enormous hits, one right after the other, fueling nonstop touring of sold-out houses on the chitlin' circuit clubs and big inner-city theaters, sometimes two or even three shows a day, either as a stand-alone act or part of a bill with other rock acts.

Taking his shtick up a level, Richard seemed able to do anything while banging on the piano keys. He could lift a leg up at will, the heel of his foot a kind of third hand as his other leg stretched backward in complete geometric symmetry. He didn't merely sing a song—he blew it apart and left it all over the walls and floor, embellished with falsetto primal screams that came out as a vibrato "*wooooo!*" as in "Tutti Frutti aw rooty, *wooooo!*" Or "Keep a-knockin' but you can't come in. Come back tomorrow night and try again, *wooooo!*" It was more than a squeal. Charles Connor noted, "He used to admire Mahalia Jackson, the gospel singer, and that's where he got that 'whooo!' He was crazy about her."

He sometimes chucked his baggy suits for campy garb he would buy from costume shops. One night Richard dressed up as the Queen of England, the next as the Pope, although it didn't take long for him to doff his own apparel and strip down to a bare chest, hurling items of clothing back into the crowd, as if in exchange for the intimate wear hurled onto the stage by overheated women.

"We didn't really know what was happening," said Connor, still in wonderment decades after. Looking back, he recalled that the Upsetters "were ducking and shouting 'Hey!' bumping heads trying to avoid all these flying panties. We cracked up. Stopped playing, we were laughing so much. I picked a pair up on my stick and waved them in the air." He added, "You couldn't miss a beat because those bodies were always moving in time," an amazing sight to be sure. Gradually, they added moves of their own—"the first band to come out with dance steps." They would, he said, "look like a well-drilled chorus line. And when Richard, out there in front of them sweating, all that water and everything, and his hair falling all over his face—you'd get a natural high just by looking at him." At many of the shows, kids filed in after cutting classes, "just to *look* at Richard. They had never seen a man like that, with long hair and all that makeup. And the band there, playing behind him, really exciting 'em."

They were so tight that, almost comically, when Richard went to a beauty salon to have his hair cut and styled, they went with him, all of them sitting under hair dryers. Between shows they would have drinks at local bars, and when they walked down the street the band put their arms protectively around Richard as they stopped and talked with the fans.

"Everyone was happy," Connor said. "We had a beautiful time— wild parties, pretty girls, wild girls. A beautiful time."

Their chemistry and synergy—one might even say alchemy— were so perfect that it never failed to bug Richard that he would need to leave the band behind when he went to record, his belief never unchanged that as great as his records were, they never quite revealed the fullest, truest degree of head-spinning magic that was the Little Richard experience. That, he said, could only be heard, seen—*felt*—in the delirious vibes of his live act.

BUT LITTLE RICHARD was too valuable and too hot for Rupe and Blackwell to allow him to be out of the studio for very long. He had to cut his insane but profitable excursions short so that he could make his way back to J&M Studios. He did so in May 1956, to get on vinyl a B-side for the next single scheduled to come down the chute, "Rip It Up." Only two songs were recorded, the Blackwell/Marascalco "Ready Teddy" and "Heeby-Jeebies," which Marascalco cowrote with Maybelle Jackson, a Specialty staffer who had written for Guitar Slim and Jesse Belvin. Blackwell wasn't happy with the takes of it from the previous New Orleans session, or these new ones, and pushed it back for a third attempt at the next session.

"Teddy" on the other hand was a sure winner, albeit a faintly veiled remake of "Long Tall Sally," with a bit more uptempo, a roof-shaking jam by the studio cats on the break, and obligatory, gender-safe references to his "rock 'n' roll baby, she's the apple of my eye." He painted a hormonal cast of '50s teenagers as "flat top cats" and "dungaree dolls," in a joint "really jumpin'," where the cats would be "going wild." (Past R&B singers had applied similar jargon—but not to pubescents "ready to rock and roll.") "Teddy," slapped onto "Rip It Up," released in June, would be nearly as ferocious a two-sided monster as "Sally" and "Slippin' and Slidin'," "Rip" streaking to number one on the R&B chart, twenty-seven on the pop, followed by "Teddy" at eight and forty-four.

With these almost matter-of-fact successes, Richard seemed to be on autopilot. And he learned a little something about the limits of even his abilities. Despite the hits that had been cranked out in New Orleans, he had never quite reconciled being ordered to record with a studio band and not the group that soldiered with him for so long, whose symbiosis with him he deemed irreplaceable. As he would say, "[I]f Specialty had recorded me live with the Upsetters that would have been the most exciting rock 'n' roll of all."

Another reason may have been that he had begun having problems with Bumps Blackwell, whose strong personality matched Richard's. Bumps would kill takes that Richard believed were plenty good enough. And Richard was so adamant about making a change that he issued an implied threat to Art Rupe—allow him to self-produce a session, backed by the Upsetters. If he refused, Richard recalled, "I would break my contract. Rupe was really mad, but there was nothing he could do." Knowing he was over a barrel, Rupe gave in, booking a session for May 15 at L.A.'s Master Recorders.

John Marascalco, who attended the session, made the point that as unstructured and undisciplined as Richard was—ingredients that aided crucial authenticity to his wild and wonderful vocals and impromptu piano flourishes—Richard badly missed the rigid, even authoritarian production methods employed by Bumps Blackwell, who was in the studio along with Rupe but kept mum. According to Marascalco, Richard "had really started getting on an ego trip. He thought that he was God at the time, and I guess he was! It was like a blackmail session."

Perhaps out of pride, Richard had selective memories of that day, saying that he recorded three songs—another try at "Heeby-Jeebies," "Send Me Some Lovin'," and "Lucille," and that "I think those recordings are as good as the others." However, records kept by Specialty show that only "Heeby-Jeebies" was done, and that after nine arduous takes none were good enough for release.

Richard would of course be aggrieved by his production work being deemed inadequate, yet for whatever reason he did not demand the same level of authority on any ensuing Specialty session. It could have been that, once in practice, he was less than knocked-out by the Upsetters' performance in a studio environment. For Bumps, though, it provided an epilogue that "There was nobody else ever got a hit record out of Richard but me."

Indeed, the worsening vibes between he and Richard during the recording process were irrelevant; it was Blackwell's innate judgment and ear for the perfect sound that made Little Richard's prime works so instantly magnetic and dynamic. A big part of the magic, contrary to Richard's picky cavils about him, was that Bumps ignored conventional recording assumptions. While most producers would have tamped down Richard's glass-shattering loud screaming—when, Bumps said, "the needles would just go off the dial"—he let it stand, which explains why Richard's voice can be heard cracking on many records, lending even more of a live feel. Similarly, Bumps left flaws in his piano playing on a track. Often, it wasn't imperfections that led Blackwell to yell "cut," it was because there weren't *enough*.

Blackwell was always amazed at the sheer voltage that those keys produced for him. Richard could pound them so hard that Blackwell remembered at least four times that he broke thick, 80-gauge strings creating the tension of the keys, something he never saw happen otherwise in any session. Still, if Richard had realized that being a producer was beyond his ken, it no doubt made him appreciate that Bumps would be there for ensuing sessions, as he was two months later—the Upsetters again brushed aside—when Richard and the New Orleans studio crew reconvened at J&M Studio in the scorching heat of summer, for three sessions on July 30—August 1, 1956. The real work was done on the first day, when they put "Good Golly, Miss Molly," "Lucille," and the finally finished "Heeby-Jeebies" in the hopper.

The latter sessions yielded useful songs, as well: "All Around the World," "Shake a Hand," and a cover of Lloyd Price's "Can't Believe You Wanna Leave." Of them all, "Heeby-Jeebies"—with Richard barely taking a breath in belting out verses of "Gotta jump back, jump back, heeby-jeebies" and lamenting a woman who "put the jinx on me" and made him "feel so sad"—went out first, in October, getting to number seven on the R&B chart. Its B-side, "She's Got It," a Richard-Marascalco collaboration, reached number nine. Both of these tunes, however, would be quickly eclipsed when Hollywood wisely, and inevitably, came calling on Little Richard.

IN 1956, THE business of Little Richard had made rock itself a financial cash cow far beyond the walls of record labels and song publishers and into the domains of other cultural profiteers. Just as with the music barracudas, Hollywood movie producers smelled money in the bundling of hip talent who appealed to the young target audience. The first blow had been struck in 1955 when the producers of the social commentary film *The Blackboard Jungle*— relying on the recommendation of the ten-year-old son of its star, Glenn Ford—picked Bill Haley and His Comets' cover of Sonny Dae and His Knights' "Rock Around the Clock" to play over the opening credits. Then, a year later, Richard sang the title song of the 20th Century Fox musical comedy *The Girl Can't Help It*, starring sex bomb Jayne Mansfield and Tom Ewell.

This was no small-change gig; the movie cost more than a million dollars to produce and would rake in six times that much. The pro-ducer/director, Frank Tashlin, a former gag writer for the Marx Brothers, Red Skelton, and Bob Hope, at first wanted Fats Domino to sing the title song and Little Richard to perform "Rip It Up" and "Ready Teddy." But when the musical director, Bobby Troup, who had cowritten "The Girl Can't Help It," called Art Rupe for permis-sion of the songs, Rupe convinced him that Little Richard was a better bet, "because he's got a lot more excitement than Fats." Soon after, in mid-October, when Richard was in New Orleans for the session at which he recorded "Jenny, Jenny" and "Good Golly, Miss Molly," he had at "The Girl Can't Help It," lifting Troupe's rather pedestrian song to Little Richard-hood by rollicking with it. In his Georgia dialect the hook came out: "The girl can't hep it, the girl can't hep it," to hypnotic background choruses repeating it, and a fired-up break with feverish piano licks paired with Lee Allen's blaring sax.

Circulated to radio stations in the run-up to the December 1 release of the movie, when the opening came the song had gone to number forty-nine on the pop chart and seven on the R&B. As simple as the song was, Richard's rendition inspired cover versions as diverse as those as the Animals, Everly Brothers, Led Zeppelin, and Bonnie Raitt. (And, given deeper context, years later when he was out of the closet it would be included in the soundtrack of the outrageous John Waters gender-bender *Pink Flamingos*.) A second song performed in the movie was the frantic "She's Got It," recorded at a quickie September session in L.A. with the Upsetters. Cowritten with John Marascalco, the song came out as the flip side of "Hebby-Jeebies" two months before the movie, rising to number nine on the R&B chart, though both sides were stepped on by the crossover reach of "The Girl Can't Help It."

In this time frame, these two Little Richard songs at the core of the movie would break important ground for rock's charter statement—its implied advocacy of miscegenation. It wasn't because of the lightweight plot, but rather Tashlin's intercut juxtapositions of Richard's Michelangelo-sculpture of an ebony face and strategically curled, dangling hair looking radiant in DeLuxe Color. The tribal moves of Richard and the band lip-syncing the suggestive lines about girls not being able to help it swathed Mansfield as she bumped and grinded on the dance floor. Some film critics have suggested that all this was a subliminal stamp of interracial conjugation. Others have hedged that such a display was no more than a satirical jab at rock and roll as a cultural outlaw. Yet, even if this were the case, Richard's winsomeness and ability to get black and white feet moving to the groove was anything but a joke.

As it was, even in the smallest doses, the palliative of Little Richard was a white producer's dream. These films, always directed and produced by white men, weren't daring enough to cast black performers in acting roles, or to put black faces in the audiences of the night clubs they were invariably situated in. Yet Richard's minor speaking lines introducing the other rock acts—Fats Domino, the Platters, Gene Vincent, Eddie Cochran—were a cultural stride forward, and creating the feel of a live performance by artists normally heard but not seen on-screen had unleashed a series of lower-budget rock exploitation flicks, many built around Alan Freed convincing "regular"—i.e., white and upscale—people that rock and roll jiving didn't lead to juvenile delinquency. Only a month after *The Girl Can't Help It* hit screens, Columbia Pictures released *Don't Knock the Rock*, one of the most enduring examples of this genre, primarily for uniting black and white rock royalty—Little Richard and Bill Haley—on the same screen, although the lobby poster for the film not coincidentally displayed Haley (who sang the title tune) and even Dave Appell and the Applejacks, yet not a trace of Little Richard. Haley performed six songs—one a cover of "Rip It Up"—and the star, Alan Dale, five. Richard and the Upsetters were limited to "Long Tall Sally" and "Tutti Frutti."

Richard was a guilty pleasure, the key to low-budget time-fillers like *Don't Knock the Rock* earning $1.2 million. To his black base, he was almost a daemon. In September 1956, he was the headliner of a major, if now-overlooked, musical event, the Cavalcade of Jazz, the annual L.A. jazz/soul concert held in the Wrigley Field minor-league baseball stadium from 1945 to 1957, then a last one at the Shrine Auditorium in '58. In all, around 125 black singers and musicians filled out the bills through the years, some established stars like Count Basie, others the newer rock and roll acts, a sort of prehistoric "Soul Train" venue. Richard and the Upsetters made their triumphant appearance, making the rickety stadium shake.

The next vehicle for the masses would drop in September 1957, Paramount's *Mister Rock and Roll*, featuring an all-world bill: Little Richard and the Upsetters (with "Lucille" and "Keep A-Knockin'"), Chuck Berry, Frankie Lymon and the Teenagers, the Moonglows, LaVern Baker, Clyde McPhatter, Brook Benton, and the Lionel Hampton Band. However, what no one in a movie theater could have known when seeing Richard cavorting in his baggy suit and skinny tie was that this was already an outdated image—that Richard's misgivings about success at any price and any amoral allowance had taken him far out of the spotlight.

A HIGHER CALLING

I knew I had a message to say to the world outside of show business.
I was not sure what it was . . . . When I knew, I came to God.

—LITTLE RICHARD

I n the wake of the movie and the single of "The Girl Can't Help
It," Art Rupe and Bumps Blackwell chose "Lucille" as Little
Richard's follow-up single. The song was another that had formed
in Richard's head way back when at the Greyhound station in Macon, centering on, as he recalled, "a female impersonator. We used
to call him Queen Sonya." The rhythm was recycled from "Directly
From My Heart to You," one of the first songs he had written, its
rumbling bottom the beat that Richard had instructed Charles
Connor to approximate from the *chocka chocka chocka* made by the
trains that rolled through Macon; that was how "Lucille" hit from
the first note, and in Lee Allen's sax and Earl Palmer slamming the

boogie beat at a slightly slower tempo. This was by plan, as Richard and Bumps wanted to reflect Richard's more mature side now that he was twenty-five.

The lyrics of the tune, cowritten with Albert Collins (not the blues guitar great), told of a woman who "ran off and married, but I love you still," the hook being "Come back where you belong . . . don't leave me alone." Good enough, but the sweet cream was a simple flourish, Richard drawing out the name into a three-syllable "Looo-seeee-*ull*," rising to a piercing falsetto. Released in February 1957, by early spring it sat at number one on the R&B chart, twenty-seven on the pop chart, sending the B-side, "Send Me Some Lovin'," off on its own run to number three on the R&B chart and fifty-four on the pop (to be covered by Buddy Holly and the Crickets on their first album, and in time by, among others, Otis Redding, Stevie Wonder, Sam Cooke, and John Lennon).

The embers were still hot when in June came the next single, "Jenny, Jenny," kicking the pace up again to riotous levels. It was one of those songs for which Richard gifted his adoptive father Enotris Johnson a writer's credit even though the lyrics were little more than revolving chants of "Jenny-Jenny-*whooo*-Jenny-Jenny" with the objective "won't you come along with me." The formula was still so solid that by the fall it peaked at number two on the R&B chart, ten on the pop. Its flip side also took off, closing a long-open circle by finally giving a ride to "Miss Ann," his long-ago paean to Miss Ann Howard, the kindly owner of the Tic Toc Club, with the beguiling line that Miss Ann was "doin' something no one can." Recorded as a blues ballad in the Fats Domino mold, it was one of the most deliberate Little Richard tunes released by Specialty, even with Richard's screeching and a blazing sax solo, and would chart six on the R&B and fifty-six on the pop.

In Little Richard, Rupe had a turnkey business, a tranche that seemed to have no end in sight, and with a profit margin increased by his headlock of royalty skimming. When it came to Richard's contract, Rupe had no intention to "rip it up" and pay him what he was due. But Rupe was not happy that, with Richard being guided and managed by Blackwell, he was not reaching maximum profitability through his tours. And so he pulled the rug out from under Bumps, removing him as Richard's manager/booker, which had been a clear ethical conflict to begin with, since Bumps's objective wasn't putting money in Richard's pocket as much as Rupe's, his boss. Rupe brought in a powerful figure, Henry Lewis Nash, vice-president of Ruth Bowen's Queen Booking Agency in New York, the largest black-owned showbiz booking agency in the country, which represented major black talent like Sammy Davis Jr. and James Brown.

It was a logical move for a star of Richard's magnitude. But Blackwell, who was bickering with Rupe much of the time, took it as a slight. He had been getting offers from other record labels for years but had held off, content to ride the Little Richard train. Now, with Richard feeling less attached to him, Bumps figured the time was ripe. Part of the equation was that the other Specialty artist he was producing, Sam Cooke, was ready to begin a solo career apart from the Soul Stirrers. Rupe was all for it, and wanted Cooke to become a rocker like Little Richard. Blackwell, however, wanted him to sing white-glove, Nat King Cole-style pop. Things got so testy that Rupe and Blackwell argued over it in the studio during a Cooke session. Blackwell then walked, signing as an A&R man and producer with L.A.-based Keen Records, taking Cooke with him. Within weeks Blackwell produced Cooke's first breakout hit, the dreamy ballad "You Send Me," which shot right to number one on both the pop and R&B charts, selling a million and a half records and turning Cooke into a heartthrob and a major superstar.

Left to fend for himself at Specialty, Little Richard would need to equal or better the stratospheric standards of his work by himself, without Blackwell's songs or direction. As self-motivated as Richard was, he had believed from the start that Bumps's role was exaggerated; that he hadn't really arranged the songs as much as that "he just copied what I was doin' on the piano." The problem was that even if he were right—a dubious proposition—life outside the studio had become even more of a deranged soap opera that would lead him to crave normalcy before he was eaten alive.

DURING THE SUMMER of 1956, Richard had met a sixteen-year-old schoolgirl of light skin and mixed race, Audrey Robinson, when he and the Upsetters played in Savannah. While a cousin of soul singer Solomon Burke, she was not a fan of Little Richard and knew little of him beyond that he was assumed to be gay. And he knew nothing of her except that, as he described it, she had a "fifty-inch bust and eighteen-inch waist." Spotting her outside his hotel, he had one of the band go out and invite her inside. "Does he know I'm a girl?" she asked the messenger. Consenting to see him, she would recall that "from the second I met him, I almost fainted. I felt weak at the knees." Getting to know each other, when Richard left for their next gig in Wilmington, Delaware, she showed up there, too. Then, when they headed for his next gig in Washington, D.C., he had her ride with him in his car—then he had her share his room in the Dunbar Hotel.

Since she was underage, no matter how womanly she looked and acted, this arrangement presented a real risk. Richard was transporting her across state lines—the very offense that would land Chuck Berry in jail in the early '60s. But such risk was common for Richard, and blithely ignored, the reward being that, as he said, she "was a wonderful lover" who "seemed to know exactly what I wanted in sex" and had "the fastest tongue in the West." Both would toss around the word "love" freely, though the relationship was stormy from the start, each volatile and stubborn. They would break up, then reunite, like clockwork. He would propose marriage, then forget all about having done so. According to Richard, their love life was, well, complicated. In the mid-'80s, he would say that he had never actually laid hands on her, that her "skills" were something he observed when passing her around to other men while sitting back and doing his own thing, literally.

One of those who spent time with her, he claimed, was Buddy Holly. As the story goes, he and Richard became friendly in 1957 when they were on the same show at New York's Paramount Theater and Buddy came to Richard's dressing room. Audrey was there and Buddy, who Richard described as "a wild boy for the women," had sex with her with Richard's blessing—during which the emcee was introducing Holly on stage. "He finished and went to the stage still fastening himself up," Richard said. "I'll never forget that. He came and went!"

Hearing of these episodes she was supposedly involved in, Audrey denied they ever happened. Their private moments, she said, were "normal," his queerness never obvious to her. "I have been around him all my life," she said. "All I can say is that I have never seen anybody except me touch Rich. . . . I guess being in the same room where people were . . . doing things . . . means I was a part of that. But Richard would never let anybody touch me. What was going on across the room was a different story." The Holly revelation? "I knew Buddy. But I didn't know I knew Buddy *that* well." And: "Richard has a wonderful imagination."

The weirdness of being Little Richard, and being *with* Little Richard, was such that—contrary to the norm in such matters—she insisted he wasn't gay and he insisted he *was*. Audrey had an enigmatic one-liner about him: "I think I was the woman that Little Richard always wanted to be," only amplifying his own caricature of himself.

In any case, whatever sort of relationship he had with Audrey—twisted, more twisted, or not—she was the first female object of love he ever had. But by mid-1957, after another proposal that Audrey rejected, she had gone her own way, taking work as a stripper and nude model in L.A. under the pseudonym of Lee Angel. Yet her place in his life, as a witness to his craziness, was nowhere near over.

IN 1957, ART Rupe had so much Little Richard product in his vault that he couldn't release new singles fast enough. Because albums did not sell as well as 45-RPM singles—not until 1968 did albums sell more than 45s for the first time—Rupe had held off on the format for Richard songs, waiting until he had a brace of hits to drive an album. Now, after six Top 40 pop and eight Top 10 R&B hits, including three number ones, Rupe went ahead with it. In March 1957, the 12-track *Here's Little Richard* was released. It was, and is, a gold mine of rock and roll's genesis, aggregating on one record "Tutti Frutti," "Ready Teddy," "Slippin' and Slidin'," "Long Tall Sally," "Rip It Up," "Jenny, Jenny," "She's Got It," and "Miss Ann," along with a few lesser cuts. (Two bonus tracks, demos of "Baby" and "All Night Long" and an interview with Rupe, were added to the 2012 remastered mix.)

Rupe guessed right. *Here's Little Richard* was an instant must-have. Although rock and roll albums were not the prized possessions they were soon to become, reaching number thirteen on the *Billboard*

Top 200 album chart was quite good for someone not named Elvis—whose own eponymous album that year spent eight weeks at the top of the chart before his album *Loving You* did the same for another ten weeks. (The other top albums were by Harry Belafonte, Nat King Cole, and the soundtracks of *Around the World in 80 Days* and *My Fair Lady.*) In the long lens of history, *Here's Little Richard* is more hallowed; in 2003, it ranked fiftieth on *Rolling Stone's* list of the 500 Greatest Albums of All Time. By any measure, even though its massive hits are available in many formats, the album is a priceless artifact of the rock era, as a chain-link of profound hits.

For Richard, it was also an added revenue stream, something always much on his mind, necessary to live like a sultan. When off the road and back in L.A., his home on Virginia Road was castle-like. Already crawling with family and friends, it was often the first destination for other elite rock and rollers who would head there when they came to town. "Mother was always cooking big dinners for all sorts of entertainers," he said, including Chuck Berry, James Brown, Jackie Wilson, and Etta James. "My sisters were young and Mother kept entertainers away from them, but they used to sneak downstairs and peek through the banisters." More impressive to the family was the income, which accrued not only from his royalty checks but cold cash he would return from tours with, stuffed into a bulging valise that he would take on the road to personally collect from promoters, which was the real reason he carried a gun.

His sister Peggie recalled, "I had never seen so much money before. I just put it on the bed and wallowed in it."

He provided for his family well. But they were not his only benefactors. At times the house was a precursor to the ATM, dispensing cash for anybody Richard had befriended. Years later, he would rue not being more careful keeping track of what was being taken. "They took everything but my clothes—and they would have stolen them if I hadn't been sleeping with my socks on! But I was having so much fun I didn't really know what was going on." Whatever it was, it seemed like it would never end. By his calculations, he was charging top dollar for concerts, each night reeling in "maybe ten or fifteen thousand dollars as our part of the total gate"—five times or more than the usual guarantee of $2,500, meaning houses were packed and jammed. At a top ticket price of only around three and a half bucks, or as little as fifty cents, his worth was astounding—all while he was swearing up and down that Art Rupe was ripping him off.

Giving so much away may have been compensation for ungodly greed. This easing of guilt was similar to his regular proposals of marriage to Audrey. Living in sin was fun, but he had a contract with the Lord and violating it was getting harder for him to rationalize. Even during the most insane of times, the inner conflict was on his mind. "When I had all those orgies going on, I would go and pick up my Bible," he said. "Sometimes I had my Bible right by my side." Sometimes, his party guests would wake up the morning after to the sound of Richard reading to them from the Bible. Trying to abide by at least *some* devout injunctions, he also kept himself dry, avoiding alcohol, weed, and harder stuff common to the music world. Still, his crazy life closed in all around him, driving away Audrey. More and more, he was beginning to think he would have to stop living halfway in sin. But to do that would require more than Richard Penniman ever believed he could do.

WITH THE LOSS of Bumps Blackwell, Richard was in the dark about how future recording sessions would unfold. Rupe hadn't consulted him about a producer to work with, and Richard assumed he would have to take charge of the process. In January 1957, his first session post-Bumps came on a whim. During a tour on the R&B circuit with the Upsetters, he booked time to cut a single song, one he had been performing for a while on the road, "Keep A Knockin'."

As Charles Connor remembered, "We were playing the Howard Theater in Washington, D.C. They had a string of theaters, like in Washington, the Howard Theater, the Royal Theater up in Baltimore, and then we would play the Apollo Theater and the Brooklyn Paramount. We did three shows at the Howard and had about a two-hour or a two-and-a-half-hour break between shows. And we went to a little studio not too far from there. It was a rush job. We only recorded the one tune. We were all cramped up in there with the drums and the amplifiers and stuff."

Despite the failure of his previous try at producing, Richard grabbed the role again with "Keep A Knockin'," which many assumed to be a response to Smiley Lewis's "I Hear You Knocking" but dated back to the 1920s and had been covered by, among others, Richard's idol Louis Jordan in 1939. Richard converted it into hard rock and roll, built around a hypnotic hook—"Keep a knockin' but you can't come in," which he spun out three times each verse, then "Come back tomorrow night and try it again." He punctuated the verses with his most feral screams yet. It was rougher, raspier, less polished, the sax solos more growling than the Blackwell-produced gems, and there was a truly fresh riff by Charles Connor as the intro, which the drummer called "the first four-bar drum intro on a rock and roll record." The riff—copied a decade later by John Bonham to kick off Led Zeppelin's "Rock and Roll"—came after trial and error.

"Richard first wanted the guitar to play the intro but didn't like it. Then he let the saxophone play it. Again, no go. And I said,

'Richard, let me do something. So I came up with a 'tat-tat-tat-tat-tat-tat-tat-tat . . .' Richard gave me a thousand dollars for that idea, and that was a lot of money in those days."

The raw power of Little Richard pulsated throughout the song, which Richard took credit for as a cowriter with the original composers J. Mayo Williams and Perry Bradford. Within weeks, it was released, zooming up the charts to number two on the R&B and eight on the pop. To Richard, it was proof that he no longer needed Bumps Blackwell or any other producer. The magic still held, his grip on his and rock's overall brand so tenacious that he now didn't need to depend on even a Henry Nash for major gigs; they would just drop into his lap. One such event came to him from Don Arden, a fast-talking British music promoter with a reputation for ruthlessness. Arden couldn't help but track American rock as it began to seep into the British music culture, something Art Rupe had a lot to do with by leasing Little Richard's records to Britain's London Records label, which distributed them worldwide, including to the Australian market, where Richard had a large fan base. Seeing the upside, Arden put together a two-week autumn "Down Under" tour, his big "get" Little Richard, who when Arden called and offered him the gig readily agreed to an offer with a guaranteed fee and generous expenses. He then added two other major American rock acts, Eddie Cochran and Gene Vincent and His Blue Caps.

However, in the interim, Richard's personal angst about the industry had him seeking reasons to make a drastic change. Charles Connor recalled that, as the summer neared, "Richard had been talking about giving up rock 'n' roll and devoting his life to God for a long time. Whenever he got down in the dumps." He had also been affected by a missionary from the Seventh-day Adventist Church, Brother Wilbur Gulley, who came to the house one day. While some regarded the Adventists as a cult, Richard listened intently to Gulley's presentation of the church's doctrines. The clincher was that one local church member of the flock was Joe Lutcher, an R&B saxophonist who had a few hits and led bands for Nat King Cole, Sammy Davis Jr., and the Mills Brothers—and was on Specialty for a time—before his own crisis of faith led him to the Adventists, and out of the business, in 1953. Gulley gave Lutcher's phone number to Richard.

When Richard called, he was struck that Lutcher's retreat was so complete that he didn't know who Little Richard was. And Lutcher was taken by Richard's sincerity.

"I was very much impressed with him," Lutcher recalled. "He told me he wanted to leave show business. In spite of all the money he was making, he needed and wanted a spiritual regeneration. There was something missing from inside him."

FIRST, THOUGH, THERE was the Down Under tour to get through. Although he had a terrible fear of flying, Richard and the Upsetters boarded a four-engine propeller plane for the long flight.

Richard was already flying high. The tour was sold out both in Melbourne and Sydney, "Keep A Knockin'" near its peak, and Rupe had scheduled another recording session for him for October 18 in L.A., at which Richard would be expected to produce more gems. The hectic, high-pressure nature of his existence combined with his inner anxieties were coming together in a perfect storm. During the flight, rather than being the usual carefree harlequin, he was quiet, tense, gripping his seat with white knuckles as he looked out the window down at the Pacific Ocean. Then, suddenly, he thought he saw something flash under the wing and began to freak out.

"This big light came over and it was frightening to me," he said, repeating what would become a familiar tale. "I could see the engines on the wings glowing red hot. I thought the plane was on fire." As Charles Connor remembered the incident, "The captain got on the P.A. system, 'Don't worry, everything will be okay because we can fly with three engines.'" But Richard was convinced otherwise, convinced he was a goner. He began praying loudly, and others joined in. When the plane landed safely in Melbourne, he was certain he'd been saved only by angels that were "flying up under the plane holding it up. It was like a sign to me."

There were more signs to come, though Richard had gotten himself together and the troupe played before deafening, teeming Aussie crowds for four days. They then packed up for the Sydney leg of the tour, held in a cavernous stadium before 40,000 people. The first show was on October 12. Richard came onto the stage to the audience wildly cheering. He sat at his piano. But before he could play a note, he had another apocalyptic vision, as he described it a "big ball of fire" shooting straight up to the sky, rising "two or three hundred feet above our heads. It shook my mind. I got up from my piano and said [to the band], 'This is it. I am through. I am leaving show business to go back to God.'"

According to some reports, he also had a sermon for the crowd, saying, "If you want to live with the Lord, you can't rock 'n' roll too. God doesn't like it."

He finished his set, not quite as frenetically as usual, then left the stage, in his mind, for the last time.

There would be numerous angles and offshoots to this interlude, all appended by Richard. One was that eight days before, Russia launched Sputnik 1, the world's first satellite shot that would orbit the Earth for three weeks. That unrelated event, in Richard's divine epiphany, was a warning to mortals—and to him directly—to repent. The satellite, that big ball of fire, was at its lowest point and Armageddon was due. It made little sense, but to Richard it all added up.

"I have always feared that the world was going to end," he confided. And if the Rapture was indeed nigh, he wanted to be on the right side.

He finished the show that night, then as he and the performers took a ferry to their hotel he repeated that this was his last show, that he would leave the tour right then and fly himself and the band back to L.A., paying the fares out of his own pocket. On the ferry, sax player Cliff Burks scoffed that Richard really was going to quit the business.

"Clifford," he told him, "if you don't believe me I'll throw all my diamonds in the ocean.'"

Then he took off his four rings—worth around $8,000—and flung them into the murky water. Burks, leaning over and trying to grab one, nearly fell off the boat.

Another Richard fable had it that the plane that brought the rest of the troupe back home ten days later "crashed into the Pacific Ocean." Of course, no such thing happened. All that mattered to him was that his return flight went without incident. That was another message, a good one. He was in God's hands now, and he'd be safe.

AFTER ARRIVING HOME, Richard did not immediately respond to inquiries from the press, nor put out a statement why he had left the tour and that he was withdrawing from the music business. This was at the urging of Art Rupe, for good reason. With Richard seemingly infallible as a hit-maker, there was just too much to be gained by his continued recording and live performances to see it all end in one fell swoop. Richard understood his position; he had every intention of fulfilling his commitment to the next session, although he would draw a line with the live gigs, as over fifty had been lined up by Henry Nash. He also agreed to keep mum for the time being, not going public with his conversion, even as stories were getting out about him cutting short his Australian appearances.

Rupe wasn't the only music mover and shaker willing to cut him slack. Don Arden, whose important tour he had left high and dry, didn't stage his usual seething tantrum when things in his purview went wrong. He wanted to stay on Richard's good side and was at least soothed a bit by the fact that few fans who had bought tickets to the last ten days of shows demanded refunds. Not dunning or crossing Richard meant he could call on him for a favor down the line.

The recording session, just six days after Richard's return, was at L.A.'s Master Recorders. It was a back-breaker. He and the Upsetters blew the roof off cutting eight songs, including covers of Jerry Lee Lewis's version of Big Maybelle's "Whole Lotta Shakin' Goin' On," as well as the Richard-penned rockers "Boo Hoo Hoo Hoo" and "Ooh! My Soul," and Willie Perryman's "She Knows How to Rock." He let them all fly as if he were on stage, as an impromptu jam session, adding the Richard touch to Jerry Lee's hillbilly standard by yipping "Shake baby shake *whooooo.* . . ." The focus of the session was to be "Ooh! My Soul," which he had already recorded with Bumps Blackwell, with mesmerizing repetitions of "baby, baby, baby, baby, baby" and "kiss, kiss, kiss, kiss, kiss," the effect like those chugging freight trains he loved, careening almost too fast for the band to keep the beat, halted only by Richard coming full stop after each verse to seductively coo the title. Feeling he had given it every drop he could, he left the studio content that he had kept his part of the bargain with Rupe.

If it were indeed to be his last session for Specialty—it wasn't—it marked the end of an era in rock that he didn't contour as much as sandblast. He then performed what would be his last live shows, or so he intended—the finale, appropriately, a triumphant gala at the Apollo Theater. Only then did he finally put out to the newspapers a brief statement about his conversion to "work for Jehovah and find that peace of mind."

And then he disappeared from sight.

Rupe never bought the Australia story, saying he believed it was "a good characterization" of something not so melodramatic, and that "the reason was other than he reveals, which is typical of Richard." His assumption was that the scenario was concocted by Richard and designed to break his contract. He may have been right. John Marascalco later told of chatting with Richard during this time, and that Richard confided that he was indeed going to study for the ministry, for two years, "then that's it," the inference being that the exile would induce Rupe to terminate the contract and then make a heralded comeback on another label.

Rupe at first wouldn't hear of letting Richard off the hook. After months had passed with no contact from him, Rupe considered Richard's continued absence from the studio and the concert stage to sell records a violation of his contract. So, he withheld Richard's artist royalties pending his return, a move with a questionable legal basis. Still, Richard didn't budge. In the context of the times, it was an act of principled independence, something like King Edward relinquishing the throne for the woman he loved. Either that or, as a highly successful black man in 1957, a cop-out, quitting while on top in an industry still restricted to and exploitative of men like him. Most simply didn't know what to make of it. His own family was shocked and worried that the money would run out. As the bankroll shriveled around them, his sister Peggie admitted, "We felt we might lose everything. We felt our whole world was going to collapse."

Leva Mae, on the other hand, supported her son's new chosen path, and seclusion. "If he had decided to change, and come to the Lord," she said, "all I could say was Amen."

seven

I'M QUITTIN' SHOW BUSINESS

I was reading my Bible, and praying. Every time I started my Cadillac I said a prayer. I was just living a life of prayer. [But] I was supposed to have been living a different life and I wasn't. **—LITTLE RICHARD**

For the now-exiled Little Richard, the plan was the seemingly impossible task of fitting in and not standing out, a complete reversion of the life he had been living since childhood. And on a romanticized level, it was surely a strong statement of pride and individualism: bowing out while on top of an industry still restricted to men like him, on his own terms and with much left to accomplish, walking away from fame and wealth for the higher priority of peace of mind. There was a definite moral subplot to his move—the man who to many in the non-rock crowd had demonic motives repenting in the most selfless way possible. Which meant he could claim with more oomph that Art Rupe *was* the devil reincarnate.

But Rupe would not begrudge him his wish to tune out and drop out. Going on the assumption that many record-buyers didn't believe, or want to believe, that rock's most electric savant was really out of the game, Rupe kept releasing Little Richard product. It was his right and, for that matter, Don Robey's as he came out of the past to issue more of Richard's R&B records backed by the Johnny Otis band on Peacock. Then there was RCA, which cleaned out its vaults of Richard's earliest and least salable ones. These artifacts sold few records but Rupe was swimming in profit as the joyful noise of Little Richard pouring out of radios and car speakers clashed with pictures of him in newspapers with his hair chopped into a neat, natural Afro style, his blinding wardrobe replaced by muted suits and ties, and even conservative V-neck cardigan sweaters, a look that rendered him nearly unrecognizable.

Despite people being able to hear his voice rocking out wherever he went, Richard was serious about becoming a minister. He enrolled at Oakwood College in Huntsville, Alabama, a traditionally black private school founded in 1896 operated by the Seventh-day Adventist Church, which pulled strings for him since he'd never earned a high school diploma. His aim was not a degree but to complete a three-year course in the School of Religion, or as he said, "to be indoctrinated." That would allow him to at least call himself a minister in the broad sense. And so, in October 1957, he dutifully packed up and drove cross-country. When he arrived at the 1,000-acre campus, heads turned. Here was the rock and roll icon in his yellow Cadillac clad head to toe in anything but sack cloth. From the start, students would gather around him, asking him to sing, a side show that the church wanted him to avoid.

Cutting him more slack, the school allowed him to take only one course beyond his biblical classes, English. But he was no more attentive in the classrooms of Huntsville than the ones he'd flunked and cut in Macon. Soon he was missing classes. Then, he and a young male student were in a dormitory bathroom where, as Richard would relate, euphemistically, "I had him show himself to me. I didn't touch him, but he went back and told his father, who was a deacon of the church." That was a double whammy, public indecency and a display of homosexual perversity, it being arguable which the church deemed as worse. Conceivably, Richard could have even been charged under arcane Alabama laws stacked against black men. Yet the church seemed more concerned with its own reputation.

At a meeting of the church board at the school, Richard bridled as the brethren tore into him. In return, "I said some nasty words that shouldn't have been said in church"—though he stressed that he was simply angered by the hypocrisy. He'd seen enough on the campus and in its offices to know he wasn't the only one engaged in such depravity. But, as he put it, "they had found out about my unnatural affections," so "I was caught point-blank and I hated it."

In the end, he said the church elders "forgave me," but that "I couldn't face it and left."

Charade that the whole thing was, Richard still maintained the appearance of change, the basis for which was at least sincere. He wanted to learn "how to love God better," not to mention himself. And the Adventists were all too happy to keep him around as a big-name human sandwich board advertising the Church of God. All they asked of him was that he either pray away the gay, or act like he was cured of it. "Everybody was telling me I needed a wife," he recalled. "They said, 'You gonna study religion, you gonna study in school, you need a wife.' And I was afraid that if I didn't marry I would go to hell."

In that spirit, he again proposed to Audrey Robinson, now known as Lee Angel, who again begged off, reasoning this time that "I didn't want to get mixed up with the church." Richard would consciously scout around for wife material, paying heavenly dues by carrying out menial church chores such as tightening the ropes at tent meetings, showing slides of bucolic places, and even "washing the feet of other members before taking communion." The high life was put in storage next to his flashy wardrobe and rich diet. "All those steaks, pork chops, chitterlings, Cokes, and coffee had to go. I ate only vegetables cooked in vegetable oils, as the church instructs."

As for the conjugal part of the bargain, that would fall into place in November when he spoke at an evangelist convention in Washington, D.C., and an eighteen-year-old college freshman of mixed blood, Ernestine Harvin, introduced herself to him. She was the prim and proper daughter of a prominent naval officer. Working in the Department of the Navy, she was as straight an arrow as Little Richard had ever known, and he so alien to her that, she would admit, "I hadn't bought his records then because I wasn't into that kind of music." But she was mesmerized by his sermon about renouncing material glory. He looked like a million bucks in his tailored suit, and he spoke in hushed, respectful tones. She brought him home to dinner where he similarly impressed her conservative parents. Thus began a long-distance romance, with not a trace of weirdness. When he brought her out for visits, she would sleep in the guest bedroom and was fawned over by Leva Mae.

But not all was so beatific. Richard would disappear for long periods of time without explanation, leaving her alone. When he put the heat on her to marry him, it was with an urgency that seemed more like something he *had* to do, not wanted to.

He was nothing if not persuasive.

To audible exhales of relief in the offices of the Seventh-day Adventist Church of God, Richard and Ernestine were engaged. In the eyes of his family, who could read him like a book, it was ill-advised. And they would be proven correct.

WHATEVER ELSE HE was doing, and with whom, the Little Richard brand hovered over the music industry like a wraith. After the success of "Good Golly, Miss Molly," Art Rupe put out three more singles in 1958, including the original Bumps Blackwell-produced version of "Ooh! My Soul" and Richard's rocking redo of the old evergreen "Baby Face." Both went Top 15 on the R&B chart and to thirty-five and forty-one on the pop, respectively, with the latter his highest-ranking record ever across the pond, going number two on the British chart, besting "Molly"'s number eight rank.

Rupe also released the album *Little Richard*, containing "Lucille," "Keep A Knockin'," "Good Golly, Miss Molly," "The Girl Can't Help It," "Send Me Some Lovin'," "Heeby-Jeebies," "Hey-Hey-Hey-Hey," "Ooh! My Soul," "Baby Face," "By the Light of the Silvery Moon," and "All Around the World." And Rupe was thinking of ways to sell Little Richard-style songs not made by Little Richard. Larry Williams, who played piano and eerily resembled Richard with his mile-high pompadour, pencil mustache, and flashy duds, had practically auditioned for this role with his song "Short Fat Fanny," in which he had name-checked Richard's hits and other early rock standards, and sang as the first lines: "I was slippin' and slidin' with a long tall Sally / Peekin' and a hidin', duck back in the alley." Produced by Bumps Blackwell, "Fanny" had done better than any Little Richard song, going to number one on the R&B chart and five on the pop in the spring of '57, selling more than a million copies. Then with Richard in exile, Williams cut two more, "Bony Moronie" in '57 and "Dizzy, Miss Lizzy" in '58, the former reaching number fourteen on the pop chart, four on the R&B, the latter hitting sixty-nine on the pop chart. Becoming a major influence on the Beatles, who performed his songs on stage and covered in recordings later on, Williams was branded with the angle that he was "finally out of Little Richard's shadow."

While Little Richard himself was deep in the shadows of his own making, Specialty would keep releasing middling Richard records regularly through 1959—"Shake a Hand," "Whole Lotta Shakin'," "I Got It" (an earlier version of "She's Got It"), and an overdubbed "Directly From My Heart to You." With so much inventory to move, Rupe also released *The Fabulous Little Richard* album. This low-grade package did include the second version of "Kansas City," which became the victim of bad timing. When Rupe finally issued it as a single, it was left in the dust at only hitting number ninety-five on the R&B chart while Wilbert Harrison's almost simultaneously released blues-rock version cruised to number one on both the pop and R&B charts, selling in the millions.

All this time, Rupe had been withholding royalties from the man who was making him so much bread. Rupe was as stubborn as Richard in not releasing him from his contract, and for most of those years had tried to keep a lid on stories of Richard's life as a music expatriate, the string of releases meant to be a counter-narrative that Richard was still actively recording. Specialty's PR people refused to answer reporters' questions about Richard's exile, even as the press would grab at any gossip about him. It was so bad that some stories claimed Richard had killed himself or was in an insane asylum. Richard himself felt he had to prove he was alive and kicking, and sane, sending out new photos of himself in his new guise, in various acts of prayer.

But Rupe was right about one thing: fame and money *did* weigh heavily on Richard's mind. Being deprived of his royalties—which had now accrued to around $11,000—based on contract abrogation bugged him to no end, and in early 1959 he filed suit in California Superior Court to recover the royalties and unspecified other income he claimed Rupe owed him. Knowing he could not bully Richard into submission, Rupe felt boxed in. Unlike Don Robey, who had forced Richard to pay up to end his Peacock contract, Rupe was too invested in the Little Richard brand, and too smart to humiliate a black superstar and risk tons of negative ink by making the same demand Robey had made. Not to mention that he was loath to have the contract and other related documents and business practices subject to lawyers' discovery. And so he proposed buying out the contract himself.

Richard and his lawyers could see right through the move. Because Rupe undeniably owed him, their feeling was that Rupe, as Richard would say, wanted to "buy me out using my own money." By mid-1959, however, when Rupe gave up the ghost and offered to settle the lawsuit by coughing up the eleven grand, Richard took it—not willing to keep paying his lawyers to keep looking for more. But for whatever reason, Richard accepted terms that Rupe asked for in exchange: keeping the publishing rights on Richard's songs and on his *songwriting* royalties thereafter, in perpetuity. As Rupe well knew, what Richard was given would be taken away by Rupe many times over. But if Richard's lawyers had serious qualms about it all, they could only recede when Richard leaped at the paltry sum of money. From his point of view, the money meant less than his peace of mind. Now, free of the Specialty headlock, he could make himself available to other record labels—exactly what Rupe had figured Richard had in mind all along rather than religion.

Rupe still could, and did, continue releasing his remaining Little Richard product, though it had become less profitable. As it was, to be able to release *The Fabulous Little Richard*, Rupe had to perform radical surgery on what were mainly unfinished chaff. On many tracks he needed to add layers of overdubbed strings and backing vocals by a female choir, and the sonic effect was not in any way rock and roll but rather a pseudo-pastoral sound. Thus, on the back of the album were mendacious liner notes that "Little Richard has added voices on several of these numbers, bringing him closer to the type of church singing he was brought up on, and to which he is now returning."

In truth, Richard had exactly nothing to do with any of this, and if he had been asked about it would have expressed adamant objections to releasing these orphaned tapes garnished by heavily echoed chorales. As it turned out, the public agreed. The album, out in March 1959, failed to chart, a clear sign that music listeners didn't feel the heat for just any old stuff with his name on it. Taken from the album, two frantic sides written by Richard, "She Knows How to Rock" (a sentence that would reappear decades later on Queen's "Crazy Little Thing Called Love") and the blues ballad "Early One Morning" (cadged from Big Joe Turner's "Wee Baby Blues") failed to chart. Same bad news with his rocking cover of "By the Light of the Silvery Moon," which copied the trend of rock groups to rework old show tunes, or its B-side "Wonderin'"— plus two more from the LP, "Shake a Hand" and his delirious cover of "Whole Lotta Shakin' Going On." To close out the year, the reworked "I Got It" and the recycled, overdubbed "Directly from My Heart to You" simply fizzled.

All of them came and went, ignored not only by America but by the man who had recorded them, who was otherwise engaged and empowered.

Downtown Macon, Georgia, circa 1940s. The busy streets were governed by Jim Crow laws, but whites often paid their way into black and tan nightclubs. This thriving scene bred three immortal Rock and Roll Hall of Famers: Little Richard, James Brown, and Otis Redding.

The childhood home of Richard Wayne Penniman, the third of twelve children, stood at 1540 Fifth Avenue, a quiet, unpaved street in Macon. Many decades later, the house was moved intact a few blocks away to Craft Street, as a Little Richard museum and community center.

Charles "Bud" Penniman strikes a carefree pose in the 1940s. A minster, bootlegger, and nightclub owner, he detested his son's effeminate ways and "devil's music" and frequently punished him with beatings and belt-whippings. They had reconciled when, in 1952, Bud was murdered outside his club.

Little Richard and his first band, the Upsetters, burning down the house before an integrated audience at Macon's Tic Toc Lounge, where he cut his teeth—and his image, here wearing a pompadour and cape. He wrote "Miss Ann" in tribute to the club's owner, who took him in when his father threw him out.

THE FABULOUS LITTLE RICHARD: Macon's Own, to head Big Annual Christmas Show and Dance at Macon Auditorium, Christmas Night, December 25, 7:00 P.M. He will be supported by Bala, The Magnificent, an Exotic Dancer of Detroit, Michigan, Annie Laurie, Blues Singer, New York City; Sylvia, Spanish Dancer of New Orleans and other great characters.

Little Richard quickly rose to local stardom, his image in newspaper ads such as this one for a Christmas show at the Macon Auditorium. In these shows before integrated crowds he shared billing with blues singers, exotic dancers, and, as the ad touts, "other great characters."

The Upsetters earned a cachet of their own backing Little Richard. Though shut out of Richard's New Orleans recording sessions, they would remain with him into the 1960s and helped break out James Brown and Otis Redding. Left to right: bassist Olsie Robinson, drummer Charles Connor, and sax players Clifford Burks and Grady Gaines.

James Brown was unknown when Little Richard urged his manager Clint Brantley to sign the raspy-voiced Brown, who idolized Richard, and stole some of his moves—and the moniker of "The Hardest-Working Man in Show Business."

Another of Little Richard's hometown stages, Macon's historic Douglass Theatre, founded in 1911 by a black man, Charles Henry Douglass. The art-deco show palace remains a favorite venue to this day for the biggest acts in rhythm and blues and rock.

After Little Richard hit like a thunderbolt when "Tutti Frutti" was released in 1955, he became the first black artist to sing a movie theme song, for *The Girl Can't Help It*. He appeared in lower-budget films before exiling from music in order to "work for Jehovah and find that peace of mind."

Revered across the pond, Little Richard frequently toured England, where audiences mobbed him on the stage with even more fervor than he had at home. Here, he mugs for the camera while hanging out backstage with another '50s American rocker, Gene Vincent, of "Be-Bop-a-Lula" fame.

Lured by promoters' lucrative offers, Little Richard toured England in 1962, his opening act the Beatles, who were thrilled to be in the presence of their idol—who at first wasn't impressed by the pre-Fab Four, but later took them to Germany to open for him there, too.

Otis Redding, who began his career as a Little Richard imitator, got his break when "The Big O" sang with the Upsetters in the early '60s, earning an audition with Stax Records. He demanded "r-e-s-p-e-c-t" for all black artists before his tragic death in a 1967 plane crash at age 26.

This October 31, 1962, shot taken at the Star Club in Hamburg—the Beatles' turf—shows why the Fab Four played second fiddle to Little Richard during his tours of Europe. Although his look and attire were toned down due to his religious retreat, his raw power and infectious persona electrified audiences.

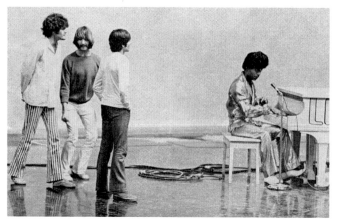

When Little Richard appeared on a Monkees TV special in 1969, they kept at a respectful distance during rehearsal as the singer-pianist warmed up, as if to give a founding father of rock his space as he went about his work.

James Brown shows off the trappings of fame during a tour of England in 1966. While he stood on equal ground with Richard on the world stage, his run-ins with the law, drug and domestic abuse, and illness contrasted Richard's knack of transporting his audiences back to their days of innocence.

The '70s were a time of profound experimentation in soul, led by Stevie Wonder and Marvin Gaye's socio-political songs like "Living for the City" and "What's Going On." The new breed of funk owed much to Little Richard, here at an awards presentation to Stevie, with Stevie's mother Lula Hardaway.

Jimi Hendrix was an itinerant guitar player when he joined Little Richard's band in the mid-1960s. The two copied each other's styles, but Richard was loath to share the spotlight and after two years of clashes, they parted, clearing the way for Hendrix's tragically brief reign as a rock god.

Richard's inner devils and lifestyle excesses could never be tamed. When he became a victim of cocaine abuse in the 1970s, the telltale signs of dissipation began to creep in, such as here during a concert in Stockholm.

Reverend Richard Penniman, during his second religious exile, would twice be unsuccessful staying away from rock and roll. Holding a picture of himself from his wild days in this 1981 shot, his impish grin hinted that, given his enduring legend, he would soon be singing "Tutti Frutti" again.

When he returned to the public eye in the mid-1980s, Little Richard traded his outrageous outfits for fashionably hip suits—able to afford them after Michael Jackson acquired rights to some of Richard's songs, and paid him $4 million to make up for some of the income denied him for decades. He wrote on this PR photo: "God loves and cares for you. Please don't forget that."

Even a near-fatal car crash in October 1981 couldn't keep Richard down. Nursed back to health in the hospital, Bob Dylan sometimes at his bedside, he made a miraculous recovery and was soon regaling the press with his usual vigor and blinding smile.

Three decades after they had embedded themselves on rock and roll's Mount Rushmore, Little Richard, flanked by Chuck Berry and Bo Diddley, appeared in director Taylor Hackford's 1987 documentary marking Chuck's 60th birthday, *Chuck Berry Hail! Hail! Rock 'n' Roll.*

John Barrett / PHOTOlink / Alamy Stock Photo

After heading the inaugural class of inductees into the Hall of Fame in 1986, Little Richard was on hand for subsequent inductions, here jamming with fellow legends George Harrison, Dave Edmunds, Mick Jagger, and Bob Dylan at the 1988 award dinner.

Susan Ragan / Associated Press

At the 1989 Hall of Fame awards, when his legatees Otis Redding, Stevie Wonder, the Temptations, and the Rolling Stones were inducted, Richard did a stirring duet with Mick Jagger, who once sat transfixed in front of the stage watching him perform during his 1963 tour of England.

Another magic moment at the 1989 ceremonies: Little Richard inducted Otis Redding into the Hall of Fame, both relaying his hometown scion's history and warbling some of Redding's most famous songs. He then presented the Hall's statuette to Otis's widow, Zelma, whom he called "Zelda."

Clad in a spanking white commodore's suit, Little Richard acknowledges the crowd's applause after receiving a Lifetime Achievement Grammy in Los Angeles on February 24, 1993. An acrid irony was that, in his prime, neither Richard nor other black performers were considered for Grammy awards.

Little Richard was on hand in Cleveland for the Hall of Fame's official opening on September 1, 1995, sharing the ribbon-cutting festivities with Yoko Ono (center) and Jann Wenner (left), Hall of Fame chairman and *Rolling Stone* publisher.

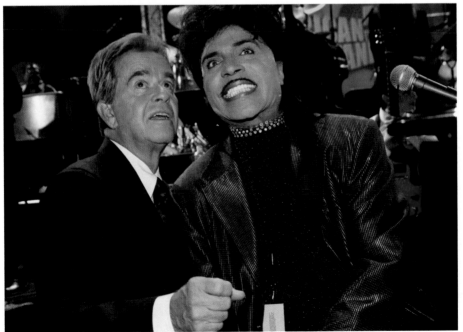

On April 21, 2002, age seventy but looking twenty years younger—as did "America's Oldest Teenager" Dick Clark—Richard rock and rolled on *American Bandstand*'s 50th anniversary TV special, its centerpiece an all-star jam around Richard's piano, everyone singing "Keep A-Knockin'."

Fats Domino visited Little Richard in his dressing room after Richard performed in The Domino Effect tribute concert at the New Orleans Arena on May 30, 2009. The two octogenarians recorded their biggest hits in the same New Orleans studio. Fats died in 2017 at 89; Richard passed in 2020 at 87.

*   *   *

ON JULY 11, 1959, Richard and Ernestine tied the knot at the house on Virginia Street, surrounded by his mostly skeptical family and friends who had to bide time until Richard came stumbling in six hours late, not a great omen. His brother Charles recalled, "I wasn't happy at all about the marriage," believing that the Adventists were using Richard and Ernestine as props to promote themselves. Based on appearances, however, all seemed good.

Like Audrey, Ernestine would tell of living a conventional, moral home life with normal conjugal relations—no outlandish scenes or Richard tending to his own satisfactions. As Ernestine would clarify, "If he was gay, he was very good about hiding it from me!" The blinding clothes he had in the closet and sexual ambiguity of his past life, she said, were "gimmicks" to make money, part of an "act" that she accepted, even if he was supposed to have renounced all that.

They spent days studying the Bible and praying. She would attend every one of his sermons, at which he never had to plead for a witness, there being swarms of fans there to see him preach and sing hymnals, some leaving disappointed he didn't put on a concert of his hits. He kept the faith. When a newspaper or magazine wanted to interview him about his recession, he insisted on being photographed in deep thought, intently reading a Bible or gazing heavenward, prayer shawl around his shoulders. Reverend Penniman—he asked not to be addressed as Little Richard—claimed he would never pick up a copy of the trade papers, or even switch on a radio unless it was to listen to a religious station. But the facade of quiet, simple-pleasured conformity and religion-based guidance started to unravel within months.

During that time, he took small but tantalizing steps to creep back into the business. He convinced Joe Lutcher to pick up his sax again and they formed a gospel-singing tandem called the Little Richard Evangelistic Team, taking road trips and making the rounds of tent shows. They pulled in handsome fees preaching and performing gospel songs, almost all of the proceeds going to the church.

While this at least seemed in keeping with his dictum to sing only for the Lord, a safe distance from the sinners of rock and roll, it still put him in close quarters with distinctly secular people. Ernestine didn't know who was worse, the religious elders or the barracuda showbiz types. Either way, they claimed too much of his time, leaving her to feel abandoned. On their way to a honeymoon, he took time to have a business meeting. Often they were strangers to each other. And it would only get worse. There were many reasons why he had less time for Ernestine. But each day made it more apparent that he was thinking about returning to the business he had forsaken. Indeed, looking for rationales, he would stress that one positive aspect he had gleaned from the brief Oakwood interlude was that he had "studied about how you can praise God through music," and that "I never cut music out of my life because music is my life, my whole life. I live for it. It's beautiful how you can talk to people through music," to the extent that his music could heal the sick, raise the dead, and make the little girls and boys talk out of their heads.

Moving inexorably toward recording again, word broke in the summer of 1959 that Little Richard was making some sort of comeback after he had won his freedom from Art Rupe. He didn't definitively know if he could record on the same high level, but he wasn't aiming for the moon anyway.

Of course, record executives would have leapfrogged each other trying to bankroll a comeback to rock and roll. But Richard's concept was very different—a pure gospel album, which he thought would work well within his gospel-rooted style. Whether or not this was fully understood by one of his targets, George Goldner—the man responsible for soul and rock music building-blocks like the Crows and Frankie Lymon—the impresario signed him to a limited deal for one album and an undetermined number of singles to be released on End Records. Hardly a salve for his ego and brand, the contract was standard, with the usual half-cent royalty structure and the co-option of publishing rights by Goldner. To be sure, walking away from the business for two years was not a boon to his bargaining power.

Indeed, few among the public knew there even was a Little Richard album on the way, which did at least permit him to work without fanfare, attention, or money, of which there was only enough as an advance to finance rather threadbare sessions. When Richard again crossed the country and went into a Broadway studio, it was without the Upsetters or any working band; the only other musician known to be involved was the gospel organist "Professor" Herman Stevens, whose '50s albums have been credited with helping to give gospel a funky beat, most centrally *Gospel Organ Music with Piano & Vibes*. Pointedly, one song Richard chose was a cover of one of Elvis Presley's "sacred" songs, "Milky White Way," which came out in 1957 and would appear through the years on three Elvis gospel albums, the first being *His Hand in Mine* in 1960. Richard, in fact, held up Elvis's gospel deviation, which also marked his Christmas albums, as a model for successful crossover. Both he and Elvis could surely ignite a church stomp or torch ballad, and Richard put as much fire and lots more nuance into no less than twenty tracks, his voice darting from bellow to vibrato, to just the organ and a backing choir, all bathed in thick echoes. He came away with his throat so raw he could barely speak above a whisper.

The problem was that, in Richard's case, singing for the Lord lacked the fun he unleashed singing for the devil. He was *too* real, too serious a disciple, whereas Elvis never cast himself as a full-time gospel singer and the feel was not far from one of his gushy love ballads. Richard chose the material with great care. Some he had sung as a child, like the Civil War-era "Just a Closer Walk with Thee," a standard of New Orleans funeral dirges, and more modern pulpit fare like "I'm Trampin'," which he sang in an unnaturally low key—but it had little appeal beyond that of a Sunday morning mass singalong. Gauging the response, he first released four tracks as singles, including "Milky White Way," to almost no attention. Then, early in 1960, he bundled ten tracks into an album, *Pray Along with Little Richard*, with Richard on the cover in the pulpit in a black suit, eyes gazing heavenward. Goldner hoped it had novelty value. It didn't. Without any outlet for it on the radio and no personal appearances by Richard to support it, few copies were bought, with most winding up in the back bins.

Giving up, Goldner quickly unloaded the remaining ten tracks in *Pray Along, Volume 2*—the final track of which was, appropriately, "I'm Quittin' Show Business," which came in two parts, the first an original number followed by a mostly spoken-word rendition of a stem-winding sermon, beginning, "I am the way of the truth and the light. I gave up ten thousand dollars a day to walk this way." Still finding few takers, Goldner washed his hands of Little Richard. (Some of the songs would later be rereleased after Goldner sold off End Records in the early '60s.)

The dismal failure of this experiment seemed to prove that, if the public had lost its appetite for Little Richard as a rocker, it never had any appetite for him as a gospel singer. This stung Richard, and sent him back into seclusion, once more adrift, a man proverbially without a country. A lost soul, and worse, a lost soul man. He seemed to carve this out when he sang what came off like a self-fulfilling prophecy (and some irony in light of the current parlance), the first lines of "I'm Quitting Show Business":

I'm quitting show business, wanna go straight
I'm gonna serve my Lord before it's too late

This was contradictory, of course. The mere act of recording an album was by definition show business. And if he was satisfied that he had gone straight before it was too late, he would soon find that the seductions and moral conundrums of sinful diversion would beckon him again, from a continent away.

eight

IN AND OUT OF THE SHADOWS

I went to England and I felt good because the Beatles brought me to England. I gave them their first tour before they made a record. I carried them to Hamburg, Germany, to the Star Club. I was the star of the show, and by the way they used to order a lot of steaks and I had to pay for them because they didn't have the money. I gave Mick Jagger his first tour with the Rolling Stones. **—LITTLE RICHARD**

By the dawn of the new decade, when a new, young president would take office and transition was in the air, the Little Richard phenomenon was in mothballs. Even Larry Williams, Richard's most successful imitator, fell hard. That year, he was busted and convicted for dealing drugs and sentenced to three years in prison. For the first time in half a decade, the Richard brand was nowhere to be found on the charts or in the press save for periodic, perfunctory dispatches about his exile. It seemed quite palpable that the Little Richard chapter of rock and roll had been concluded. If so, Richard could feel justifiably proud about what he had wrought, which Elvis had magnified to a level thought unimaginable only three years earlier.

Few could have foreseen that when Little Richard screamed *a-wop-bop-a-loo-mop-a-lop-bam-boom*, such indeterminate English would be the glue of rock and roll lyricism, holding together the guts of songs needing to fill syllables—for example, "Yip yip yip yip yip yip yip yip / Bum-a-mum-mum-mum-mum, get a job." Even a parody of the novelty, "Who Put the Bomp," was a huge hit. This new hipster lingo could be heard every day on the radio and also on TV shows geared specifically for the rock generation, the turning point being the after-school ritual of *American Bandstand*, its host a Philadelphia disc jockey, Dick Clark. Yet, coincidental or as a natural progression, the lost years of Little Richard only added to the loss of verve in American music. When Richard quit, he left a thriving industry, the echoes of him far and wide, in the work of Larry Williams, Long Tall Marvin's "Have Mercy Miss Percy," Bobby Darin's "Queen of the Hop" (the melody taken from "Slippin' and Slidin',"), the Del Vikings' "Flat Tire" ("Lucille"), Don Covay's "Bip Bop Bip," and even rockabilly songs such as Jimmy Dee and the Offbeats' "Henrietta," another cop of "Lucille."

In England, ska and skiffle were converting to yowling Little Richard-style rock, which they called "beat music," with pasty-faced boys trying to sound black on songs such as "Shakin' All Over" by Johnny Kidd and the Pirates. As Richard would say, "It flattered me—but it also annoyed me because it went on and on." In America, however, aboriginal rock was dimming. Before Larry Williams went to jail, his cover of "Heeby-Jeebies" was a flop. Down in New Orleans they kept pumping out Fats Domino hits and other gems like Huey "Piano" Smith and the Clowns' "Don't You Just Know

It," Frankie Ford's "Sea Cruise," Joe Jones's "You Talk Too Much," and Ernie K-Doe's "Mother-In-Law." But Nashville had caught up with country-flavored white rock by acts like the Everly Brothers and Roy Orbison, whose aching vulnerability painted an entirely different portrait of manhood than that of Little Richard.

Atlantic's Jerry Wexler would later say of the forlorn state of pop music, "Primitive, booting rock 'n' roll was losing ground in the marketplace. Elvis Presley was in the Army. Little Richard was in the ministry. Jerry Lee Lewis was in disgrace and Buddy Holly had died a tragic death [in the 1959 plane crash that also killed Ritchie Valens and the Big Bopper]."

In retrospect, one can justifiably fault Little Richard for ducking out instead of playing a lead role in transitioning to a new era. And it was surely to rock's detriment that he wasn't there to compete with Sam Cooke or Jackie Wilson, whose gravity-defying, acrobatic moves earned him the moniker of "Mr. Excitement"—another handle that would have been perfect for Little Richard. Despite his withdrawal, Richard's legacy was sill palpable. In Macon, Otis Redding was following in his footsteps—although Richard's boast that Otis "was in the business because of me" is a stretch, the connection being Redding's brief time with the Richard-less Upsetters before he earned an audition with Stax (where one of his early songs, "Shout Bamalama," was a cover of Little Richard's "Bama Lama Bama Loo"). With regard to Little Richard, though, there was a very real question about whether he belonged in any corner of music.

RICHARD HIMSELF DIDN'T share those doubts. Rather than giving up on his now-tenuous foothold in the business, he sized up the failure of his "sacred songs" for George Goldner and was convinced that he could still make such songs fly to a certain segment of the market if he could work with a skilled producer. Looking for another home in the industry, he found a taker that seemed to check all the right boxes. This was Mercury Records, the giant Chicago label that made its mark with a roster of jazz artists, one of whom was conductor and arranger Quincy Jones, who in his late twenties had already been around the world as musical director for Dizzy Gillespie, living for a time in Paris as head of Mercury's French record label. He had just moved to New York when the Mercury brass signed Little Richard to record another album of religious music; Jones was assigned to be the album's musical director. And, as it happened, Jones was tight with Bumps Blackwell, in whose jazz band he had played trumpet in the late '40s when Jones was sixteen.

Blackwell had made some major changes in his own life. After riding high with Sam Cooke, in 1959 he split with the artist, who had jumped again, to RCA. Blackwell signed with Mercury as its A&R director. That Quincy could reunite Bumps with Richard clinched the deal, leading Richard to hire Bumps again as his personal manager once the project would be completed. That was all Richard expected to do, the deal—as with End—contingent on the success of one album of gospel material, and Jones was just as pumped about it. He would later say of the June 1961 sessions in New York, "I can recall none that moved me more," and shared Richard's skew that "he was more than just an entertainer, he was a true believer. [H]e wasn't just singing it. He was preaching it . . . the cry of a triumphant man [who] had been saved. All of us in the studio were deeply moved and impressed." Before the album's release, he wrote ads for the trades hailing it as a "long awaited one by everyone. Rock 'n' Soul is here to stay!"

That was how Mercury wanted it to be positioned, not as gospel as much as Richard redefining rock and soul by taking it back to its gospel roots with a contemporary beat. This seemed a logical aim, given that Richard warmed up for the Mercury album by recording some tracks with the Upsetters for a proposed album by the band, though insisting his name be kept off it. And in the studio, Bumps gave it all he had trying to reach that highest ground. The album, *Little Richard, The King of the Gospel Singers*, included original songs written by Richard ("He's My Star") or ones cowritten with Jones ("Do Lord, Remember Me" and "Ride On, King Jesus") or William Pitt ("He's Not Just a Soldier"). The balance was filled out by standard gospel like "Joy, Joy, Joy (Down in My Heart)" and Thomas Dorsey's "Peace in the Valley," which Blackwell had produced for the Soul Stirrers and had been sung by Elvis on his third Ed Sullivan appearance. Richard revered the song because of Mahalia Jackson's 1937 version, singing it regularly on stage, and when she heard his take in the '50s said she was "delighted" that he gave it "a primitive beat" and was "the way church music should be sung."

Allotted a big budget, Blackwell brought in a forty-piece orchestra to embellish Jones's own band, as well as the Howard Roberts chorale. (Roberts, a tenor soloist of spiritual songs, also played trumpet in Lionel Hampton's band, was musical director for Cab Calloway, and was a Broadway actor whose credits included *Porgy and Bess*.) Given the heavyweights in the studio, and Richard's rebirth as a mannerly messenger of the Lord, the assumption was that he was over his wild days and temperamental flights. But early on, he showed up late for sessions, making a full room of musicians sit around, their hourly union pay accruing. Then, after he had dropped off a friend at the bus station, he went into the men's room to, as he would put it, "watch people take [them] out and urinate." Perhaps doing a bit more, he was—shades of his time at Oakwood—arrested and wound up paying a fine to drop the charges.

Once in the studio, though, he was all business, and the quality of the work was vastly superior to the amateurish feel of the End songs. "He's Not Just a Soldier," the first song released as a single, was a trenchant parable of the moral dilemma of soldiers in war, with a dramatic military-style "hup, tup, thrup . . ." prefacing Richard's memorable, emotional hook, "He's not just a soldier, he's one of God's sons." "He's My Star" was an ethereal flight, the vocal reaching high on a cloud of violins then dissolving into the ether. "Do Lord, Remember Me" was a pure gospel foot-stomping, hand-clapping shaker, Richard sliding up and down the scale with his voice, laying down, "No man can hinder me . . . for He is King, my Lord." Indeed, his broad range and effortless changes in key and mood were remarkable, sounding like a different witness on each track.

Overall it was a valiant and sincere effort, and the album would endure as a real step forward for secular singers needing to unburden with the salve of gospel. Released in August 1961, the cover pictured Richard, his fists clenched and his face intense. Its songs were Richard's first to be mixed in stereo. On a broad plane, it was a niche item with only incidental rock and roll appeal, but "Soldier," when released in September with "Joy, Joy, Joy" as the B-side, was able to get to number 119 on the pop chart. Seven years later, at the height of the Vietnam War protests, "Soldier" would be covered by Thomas Douglas, who added a blunt spoken-word intro and sound effects to amplify the corrosive horror of war.

Two more singles, "Ride On, King Jesus" with its B-side "Do You Care" in January 1962 and "He Got What He Wanted (But He Lost What He Had)" in May 1962, didn't do as well, although they were heard, and like several of the album's tracks, remembered. And despite its lack of mass appeal, or a place on the charts, for Richard it was a boon, its overwhelming positive reviews making clear two distinct and interrelated realities—one, that his withdrawal was not, as Art Rupe suggested, a ruse; and two, he was still serious about recording and playing live gigs. The album, Richard admitted, "was the thing that really put me back in business," the best part being that "it was just the kind of music I had always wanted to record."

After Richard invited Mahalia Jackson to hear him sing at the Mount Maria Baptist Church in L.A., Bumps Blackwell put them together on a nationwide tour of churches and religious convocations, which for Richard was close to knowing what heaven felt like, being with the woman who would sing at Martin Luther King's March on Washington. It was also a stair-climber for Joe Lutcher, whose association with Richard led him to step back into the business, as well, opening a gospel record shop and then his own label, putting out records by gospel groups. In the wake of the album, two of the Upsetters demos that Richard had sung on to get them a record deal were rushed out on a single for producer H.B. Barnum's Little Star label, one a sped-up cover of Fats Domino's "I'm in Love Again," the other a sensuous blues ballad "Every Night About This Time." Although they were credited to "The World Famous Upsetters" the songs were implicitly marketed as new Little Richard material, although Richard was embarrassed by the rough, unpolished cuts and no doubt was relieved they garnered little traction.

For Mercury and Quincy Jones, the gamble of sinking a bundle of money into a Little Richard gospel album didn't pay off financially but was nonetheless a noble piece of work. Even as a one-off, with no further contractual obligations, it sent Richard back to the routine of seeking a big label for just such a follow-up, now with the credibility of having delivered a solid piece of work. Neither did it hurt his mission that the Upsetters tracks, such as they were, could have been an implicit clue that Richard was itchy to get back into the rock fold. These factors were enough to lead Atlantic Records to give him a deal, agreeing to a gospel album that would be followed hopefully by new Little Richard rock and roll. At the time, Atlantic was a font of highly successful white-glove soul, led by Leiber and Stoller's production of string-laden, Latin-flecked monster hits with the Drifters. The thought of perhaps teaming the duo that had helped unleash rock and roll in the studio with Little Richard might have made Ahmet Ertegun and Jerry Wexler's heads dance with possibilities.

Richard, apparently with no greater objective than gospel, went into a studio in L.A. in mid-June to cut half a dozen songs, producing them himself, aided by arranger Jerry Long conducting a full orchestra that included sixteen-year-old Billy Preston, a wiz kid who had played piano and organ for Mahalia Jackson. But none of the tracks were anywhere near completed when the project was put on hold for another Richard lane change, one that would reroute his path once again.

IN THE FALL of 1962, Richard got another call from Don Arden. The hard-boiled Brit promoter, who had let Richard slide when he walked out on the Australia tour five years before wanted to cash in on that favor. Unlike in America, the aura of Little Richard remained strong overseas—along with continued sales of his oldies, the songs "He's Not Just a Soldier" and "He Got What He Wanted" had both made the charts there—and his influence was all over the British homeboy rock bands. As Arden saw it, shows headlined by the "Architect of Rock" himself would command a king's ransom, thus he could wave a lot of money under Richard's nose in getting him to agree to his first tour of England in early October. Arden had already signed up Sam Cooke for the tour with the idea of combining all that talent in a sure windfall. And Richard was receptive, on the condition that he be the headliner, with Cooke his opening act—perhaps the only man who could have made such a demand given that Cooke was a current star and more relevant. Yet Sam out of deference agreed and the tour was on.

However, there was a serious misunderstanding.

Richard believed he and Cooke would be performing gospel tunes while Arden wanted only rock and roll.

Arden realized he had a problem when Richard, plugging the tour, spoke only about his excitement to sing for the Lord in England. Fearing this would kill ticket sales, Arden ran ads in the British press that he had booked Richard "purely as a rock artist, and his repertoire WILL consist of old favorites like 'Rip It Up' and 'Long Tall Sally.'" His conclusion was as overblown as it was profound: "Little Richard is back in business and has chosen Britain as the base from which he will launch his comeback bid." Considering Arden's reputation for making deals based on false promises that he would later bluster and bully his way out of, it is entirely possible he'd conned Richard, who operated on the assumption that he would be singing gospel.

Rather than take the chance of another "Sputnik" moment, Richard didn't fly to England but rather set sail on an old ocean liner called the Rotterdam, taking Preston with him as the only musician he thought would be necessary. He found the conditions so awful on the ship that he would pun, "It was dam' rotten all the way." To pass the long hours, he sang hymns and preached sermons on the deck. He got to England a day before the opening show, on October 8, at the Gaumont Theatre in Doncaster, the first of two performances there before he would hopscotch the country for thirty-nine shows over three weeks. Not knowing of Arden's vows to the public, he got to Doncaster prepared to go out and do his old-time religious songs and raps, looking every bit like a minister, his hair short, his frame wrapped in a flowing robe, the effeminate shtick and batted eyelashes just a memory from *Don't Knock the Rock*.

Arden was already in a snit. Cooke's flight to England was delayed and he missed the show, sending Richard on right away. And when he entered in his robe, no one in the packed house quite knew what to think.

Then, backed by Preston's dulcet organ, Richard launched into his sacred songs and devotionals, leaving the house baffled about what they had seen. Arden, who hadn't seen or spoken with Richard before he had gotten to England, was beside himself during the show, ranting that Richard was going to ruin the whole tour and that he might have to pull the plug on what had ballooned into a sold-out enterprise—and issue refunds, taking an immense loss. He did catch a break in that there was no one from the rabid British music papers at the first show, sparing him immediate pain. Knowing there would be critics at the second show of the evening, Arden figured he had one shot to make things right. Getting in Richard's face, he pleaded, cajoled, and tough-talked him to sing his hits. But Richard was adamant.

By then Cooke had finally arrived and Arden appealed to his manager, J.W. Alexander, who had worked at Specialty and was friends with Richard, to change Richard's mind. Alexander said it wasn't necessary, since Cooke would go on before him and sing his hits. Competitor that Richard was, he would want to crush him. And he was right. Watching Sam rip it up from the wings, getting people dancing in the aisles, Richard told Preston he would be singing his hits. He doffed his robe, revealing the alabaster white suit he wore under it, and in the dark hall he tiptoed out and began noodling on the piano in time with Preston's organ. Then, with the audience titillated, with no intro or orchestra the lights came on and there he was, illuminated in white, diving right into "Long Tall Sally." The showmanship was nonpareil, the performance a stripped-down but uncompromising Little Richard, evoking raw emotions and uninhibited exhilaration in a crowd of white Brits, most of whom had heard but never seen black American rockers.

Arden's money spigot was back in business. He could happily tout the rest of the tour as Little Richard's comeback, the weird irony being its location, an ocean away from where he had reached the summit. In this context, nobody was more responsible for this turn of fate than Sam Cooke, for keeping Richard's competitive fire burning. More and more comfortable with this implied return to secularity, Richard loosened up each day, performing with not only Preston but the band hired to back Cooke, Sounds Incorporated, and leaping about like a jumping bean, doing his stripteasing, even vaulting into the crowd, an old Richard trick that can be seen as the seed of stage-diving. He also recycled the bit that James Brown had lifted, falling in a heap as if lifeless, lying motionless as a worried roadie stood over him, and as the crowd went silent, then bolting up like a rising phoenix to finish the song. Every song was coordinated with the lights being cut or turned up to blinding glare. Most significantly, he was loving every second of it, the king once more.

And, as it happened, a kingmaker.

EVEN BEFORE WORD would get back to America that Little Richard was more than ready to rock again, back home there were more pressing matters going on, the gripping tension of the Cuban Missile Crisis rising all that month before mercifully ending peacefully. But across the pond, the comeback king would open the gate for the Beatles to become the *Beatles*. As it happened, the reviews and word of mouth spilling from the tour were quite pertinent to managers of local bands that had been bred by Little Richard. The Beatles at the time were rising, having had their first hits in the U.K. But they were pretty much an itinerant group bouncing from the underground rock clubs of Liverpool, most famously the Cavern Club, and the red-light district of Hamburg, Germany—which George Harrison called "the naughtiest city in the world." While they were honing their sound, they were also getting into fistfights with likewise inebriated punks, inhaling uppers to play long into the night, hanging in brothels, crashing on floors flooded by broken toilets, congealing their lineup with Ringo Starr, and adopting their cereal-bowl-styled hairdos. Also getting deported for various offenses.

After the puckish, calculating Brian Epstein became their manager, Hamburg again entered the picture, with a Little Richard connection.

Epstein, who owned a record store in London, was friendly with Don Arden and frequently attended the promoter's concerts. Catching a typically dazzling Little Richard performance, Epstein was more than willing to have his band open for him, to reap the publicity rewards. Richard had no idea who they were, but Epstein told him, "These boys worship you." This was no jive; when he met them, they were so tongue-tied they could barely speak. Seeing the not-yet Fab Four, Richard was unimpressed.

"I didn't think they'd make it," he recalled.

The Beatles normally performed "Lucille" and "Long Tall Sally" in their concerts; now, still in awe of him, they chose not to sing them lest they offend him. But Epstein kept working him. According to Richard, "Brian said to me, 'Richard, I'll give you fifty percent of the Beatles. Take the masters back to America with you and give them to the record companies for me.'" While this sounded like another dollop of pure Richard blather, it was true that the Beatles had no record deal in America at the time—though the notion of Epstein ceding half ownership of the Beatles to get one is preposterous. In any case, Richard said he declined the half-interest but promised to make some calls on Epstein's behalf. The Beatles' manager still wasn't ready to let Richard go. He added two more Liverpool gigs, at the Tower and Empire theaters, again with the Beatles as a warm-up act. And after that, Arden had one more offer, booking Richard on a fourteen-night tour of the Hamburg clubs through late November, the motive for Epstein being to extend the Beatles-Richard relationship on more exotic turf. As Richard would tell it, "I took the Beatles with me," as if they were nominal performers needing charity when in reality the Beatles had become quite popular in Hamburg on their own, enough—following their previous deportation—to be allowed back into Germany for the engagement.

Even so, Little Richard's presence and input given to the Beatles as entertainers was of no small value. Spending long hours together, the Beatles followed him around like lap dogs, breathing in his chatter about the industry and rock, making mental notes of the advice he handed down about stage craft and the art of singing without losing spontaneity or honest emotion. They couldn't get enough of him. When the subject of their discussions wasn't music, they'd pepper him with questions about America and California in particular. To him, they were boorish, bumpkins, rubes with funny Cockney accents. "They'd come to my dressing room and eat there every night. They hadn't any money, so I paid for their food. I used to buy steaks for John."

Paul, who would always sit closest to him, would tell him, "Just let me touch you."

Said Richard: "He wanted to learn my little holler, so we sat at the piano going 'Oooooh! Oooooh!' till he got it." Only then would the Beatles sing Richard's songs with conviction. On "Long Tall Sally," which they had never gotten quite right, Richard took more credit. "I taught Paul the guitar part," he said, even though Paul by then had long switched to playing the bass after Stu Sutcliffe quit the group and stayed in Germany. To be sure, Paul's mastering of the Little Richard primal scream can be heard on the cover of "Sally" on the late-seventies album of tapes made by a stagehand of a Hamburg show and released on a German label as *Live! at the Star-Club in Hamburg, 1962*. And Richard quickly amended his original doubts about them, surprised that these hicks had an abundance of talent, could hit a hardcore rock groove that paid homage to him, and most impressively, were also convincing as an R&B band.

With his admiration also came the natural competitive fire within Richard when he played on shows featuring the likes of Chuck Berry. (Witness the time he set actual fire to his piano before Chuck had to do his set, yet another rock precedent.) Sensing he must put the Beatles in their place, he turned up the heat to scenery-melting levels when he hit the stage. Preston, who had a front-row seat for it all, confirmed that "it was exciting because you never knew what he was going to do. . . . He put everything into the show [and] knew just how to get the kids going." Only one of the performers on the stage at the time was mobbed, often, by crowds that would be so worked up they would surge onto the stage, tearing away at his clothes, leading him to have to borrow shirts from others—one being Paul McCartney—and cuff links, which would also be lost. One show had to be cut short when security couldn't control the fans and formed a phalanx around Richard to get him out.

Accordingly, in hindsight, he would both exalt and reduce John, Paul, George, and Ringo at once. Of his shared time in history with the Beatles, he would say, raising his voice to make the point to skeptics, "I had taught them to rock! I was their idol and they were my apprentices!"

Indeed, Billy Preston would recall that "when Richard left to go back to the United States they cried." So might have Billy. Because when Richard had seen him spending so much time around the Beatles between shows he got his back up, his proprietary ownership of any musicians he had on his payroll making such fraternization tantamount to treason, sleeping with the "enemy." When the tour ended and Billy wasn't ready to go, Richard, he said, "left me in Hamburg without a ticket home." Billy learned that his ticket had been given to Don Arden, and finally made it home, going to great lengths groveling to Richard to be taken back into his good graces.

Still, petty grumbling aside, Richard was so invested in the Beatles that he fully intended to keep his word and try to land them a record deal in America. While still in England, he had placed an overseas call to Art Rupe, who despite all the static between them had kept in contact with him hoping for a rapprochement. And Richard was all for Art getting in on the ground floor of the next big thing, pimping the band who, as Richard insisted, "can imitate anything" on the music buffet. However, Rupe, who had not heard of the Beatles and was the living archetype of old-school protocols, demurred. "Richard," he said, "I am not interested in anyone but you. I want you to come back and sing like you did before."

In the long lens of history, it was one of Rupe's dumbest decisions, as was Richard's declination of any financial connection—if in fact any was offered—to the Beatles. But in real time, Rupe's lingering desire to be in the Little Richard business meant that the rock 'n' roll Richard brand was alive and well, even after years of idleness. And this reality was again eating away at the moral barriers he had erected around himself.

REVIVAL

I thank God and all of the kids everywhere for the acceptance I have received. I have been in show business twenty years—since I was eight years old!—and I have sold 32 million records. And isn't it amazing . . . through all these years, the kids still know me and receive me. That can happen only to a person that the people accept. Dick Clark has been very sweet to me—he has let me come on his shows whenever I get ready, and others have been very sweet to me and let me come on their shows because I'm a legend—and I'm still alive! **—LITTLE RICHARD,** 1966

*I*n late 1962, Richard returned to America in time for the holidays, and resolved to finish the tracks he had made for Atlantic months before. New sessions took place in February and April 1963, and though these recordings nodded a bit more to rock—such as his cover of "Crying in the Chapel"—this too was a vehicle for his obsession to make gospel cool. Covering Jerry

Long's "Hole in the Wall," his wry manner made him sound like Brook Benton, with a sprightly choir and pop-like hooks accented by clever violin runs. The traditional gospel shouter "Travelin' Shoes," driven by Billy Preston's pyrotechnic organ, was a part-rap sermon. With nothing of his own to record, Richard threw in a latter-day valentine to Leva Mae, his take on "My Mother's Eyes," bathed in lush gospel overtones, though it would not be released and lost in history.

He was still keeping to his self-imposed exile from rock and roll while in America, and had not been deterred from completing his studies at an L.A. college toward a bachelor's degree in theology and minors in psychology and business—the three areas not incompatible in his unique world view. But it seemed that whenever he had made peace with himself again about the purity of his soul, the gospel of rock would again intrude. Gingerly, Richard opened the door a crack, but closed it on Atlantic; in his gut he had concluded that the label wasn't compatible with his aims and wouldn't provide the push he needed to recapture the spotlight in the States. For that, he felt far more comfortable with Art Rupe.

By the spring of 1963, Richard—paying no mind to the fact that he still had contractual obligations with Atlantic—agreed to record under the auspices of Specialty Records, albeit just one side, "Well Alright!" which Sam Cooke had written for him after a phrase Richard used as part of his sermons. Neither did Rupe commit to giving him a contract because to do so would require him to buy out Richard's Atlantic contract. On a purely look-see basis, Richard went into Cooke's L.A. studio, which Sam permitted him the use of gratis for the session. But with no serviceable song as a B-side, Rupe would sit on "Alright," though in retrospect this was precisely what record executives wanted from Richard: his joyous pulpit shouting fitted with a booming rock beat and having no specific references or appeals to the Lord. The title was a sizzling hook for Richard's lead vocal and an accompanying girl-group-style backup, the vibe copied by the "Movin' On Up" theme song of the *Jeffersons* TV show in the '70s.

Rupe waited for Richard to follow up with more material but would need to wait longer. In the summer, Don Arden rang up Richard with another well-paying offer, to come over and headline one more tour of English concert halls by American rockers to stretch through the fall. Arden had made a go of it with Bo Diddley and the Everly Brothers as the tour's big names and British bands as warm-up acts, including the blues-loving Rolling Stones. But ticket sales lagged and Arden figured Little Richard would pump the tour up. For Richard, it also pumped up his ego and bank account. Having come to depend on the European market for almost all of his income, he upended his life again, taking Billy Preston once more on the long trip to England, again leaving Ernestine in L.A.—a habit that had put a serious cleft in the marriage. Constantly hoping he would fulfill his vows to live a simple life, she knew now that was not in his nature.

"Being around people and doing things and being the center of attention," she would say, "is part of his makeup. If you take that away, you're going to hurt him."

Letting the open wound in the relationship fester, and with both knowing the sham marriage was on life support, Richard was on the stage and ripping up concert halls in late September. A review of an October show at the Gaumont Theatre in Watford, "RICHARD IS DYNAMIC," opined that he had "proved that he is still the greatest, wildest performer on the beat scene. Every Little Richard hit from 'Lucille' through 'Good Golly, Miss Molly' was hurled at the audience, which stamped, raved and yelled with the artist . . . . By the end of his act, he was stripped of all clothing except blue mohair pants. After he closed the first half, the yells for an encore lasted almost five minutes! This man is tremendous." In November, he also anchored an Arden-booked show with the Shirelles and Duane Eddy at the Regal Edmonton, with the *Record Mirror*'s critic agreeing that Richard "gave a splendid performance."

By then, his arc had coincided with the Rolling Stones, who were also a year or so away from the top rung of rock and were just as transfixed as the Beatles had been bearing witness to Little Richard. Just like Paul McCartney, Mick Jagger, who called Richard "my first idol," got as close to him as he could, even sleeping on the floor of Richard's room at night; during performances, the rubber-limbed front man studied his every move from a position just off the stage as Richard, said Mick, "drove the whole house into a complete frenzy," describing the effect as "hypnotic, like an evangelistic meeting where Richard is the disciple and the audience the flock that followed." His verdict was that "nobody could beat Little Richard's stage act." Indeed, the act seemed to be in the hands of a higher power, or else Richard's acting ability. At one show, he collapsed to the floor, appearing to either be felled by a coronary or seizure. An ambulance came and he was put on a stretcher. Then, he bolted upright, jumped to his feet, went back to his piano and picked up singing "Lucille."

Little wonder Keith Richards called getting on stage with Richard that night for a curtain call "the most exciting moment of my life." And it's no surprise that it was only when Jagger learned to approximate Richard's searing vocals and his strut that the Stones broke through; on this tour, still learning, they incurred a good many boos, for which Richard would upbraid the crowds. The tour ended with a bang, a TV show on Britain's Grenada Network built around Richard and also featuring the Shirelles and the band Richard toured with in England, Sounds Incorporated, who were managed by Brian Epstein and would be the Beatles' opening act on their 1965 American tour. The show's producer, John Hamp—who needed do nothing but give Richard the cue to start playing and then have the cameras follow what was a near riot of teenagers nearly wrecking the studio—recalled it as the most wildly compelling program ever on the tube.

But Arden had more constructive work for him to do, at Epstein's prodding—to reunite Richard with the mop-top band who were again quite willing to take second billing, this despite the Beatles having become objects of worldwide fascination in the year since, mobbed by hordes of teenage girls chasing them down the streets of Liverpool. The buzz around them had led to their first records being released in America in '63—though, like Art Rupe, Capitol, the American division of the Beatles' home label, judged their records not suited to American tastes; instead, the Chicago-based, black-owned Vee-Jay label would release them, making a mint.

But Richard's own buzz could still provide the Beatles a crucial boost. They had already gained from the association, having covered "Long Tall Sally" on several early bundles (to appear later on two retrospective live albums and be the last song the Beatles performed live on stage, in 1966), and their cover of his dual versions of the same song, "Kansas City"/"Hey, Hey, Hey," would appear on two of their early albums and as the B-side of their single "Boys." To Richard's great dismay, though, his influence on them would never be fully appreciated, or even generally known, or that the wildness of Beatlemania was nothing but a rerun in his eyes of "Richard-mania" that had surrounded him a near-decade before. But Epstein knew of it, prompting him to reverse his own band's status and open for Richard on a two-month return trek through Hamburg, at the Star-Club—perhaps the only act they would have stepped back for.

They were just as respectful of him as they'd been the first time, if a bit less reverential, their own confidence and arrogance swelling their heads. Richard's respect for them was also real, and he would act as a quasi-PR man praising them in interviews. But there was also some thorniness with the boorish John Lennon. As Richard remembered, "John had a nasty personality," by example, "[He] would do his no-manners [Richard's way of saying passing gas] and fan it all over the room, and I didn't like it." Naturally, the converse was that it was never easy to be around Richard, who for all his ingratiating bluster had his own nasty streak; witness his spiteful treatment of Billy Preston the previous year in Hamburg. And Billy would not be his only protege who would feel his spite.

Next in the line of fire was a gypsy-like guitarist whose headstrong ambition and exalted sense of style and self ran smack into the unlimited vanity of Little Richard.

WHEN RICHARD GOT back home late in the fall of 1963, like all Americans he was hit in the face by the news bulletins that changed everyone's life on November 22. The young president was murdered in Dallas. Much of America died on that grassy knoll, as well, sending the world into a stunned coma, including the insular world of rock and roll that seemed to stop dead in the shroud of shock, grief, and mourning. Yet this malaise seemed to set the stage for another kind of jolt, a new order centered around the band that never again would take second billing, to anyone. That happened within weeks when Ed Sullivan brought the Beatles to America for their first tumultuous appearances on his show. By then, realizing its faux pas, Capitol reasserted its rights and released the *Meet the Beatles!* album, which sat at number one in America for eleven weeks.

Undeniably, the Beatles that came into America's living rooms on February 9, 1964, had put those tutorials from Richard to maximum effect, soaring the Brits to the aerie of rock, becoming overnight forebears of a cultural paradigm shift. Repeating Richard's blueprint, they expanded into the cultural fabric starring in the vérité-style *A Hard Day's Night.* All of which was more déjà vu for Richard. And seeing the pandemonium and mega-dollar deals accrue around his "apprentices," envy surely crept in. The "king" (or "queen") himself was only minimally on the radar screen in America. Atlantic had released four of the tracks he had cut for them, "Crying in the Chapel"/"Hole in the Wall" and "Travelin' Shoes"/"It Is No Secret," all licensed to the British and German markets, as well. But little promotion was put behind them, further undercutting the viability of the "reverend rocker," and the less gospel-like "Crying in the Chapel," though given the most promotion, could only get to number 119 on the pop list. No album of the tracks would be released (they are today available in retro-releases from Warner Music Group, Atlantic's corporate overlord).

What's more, it was still not an easy decision to step fully back into the bright lights of rock and roll. Incredible as it seems, Richard had hidden from his mother that he had re-entered the showbiz back door, telling her he was going to Europe to preach; his brother Marquette, who he took with him as his road manager, also pushed that fable, keeping Leva Mae happy that he had made his peace with the Lord permanent. Not that Ernestine was fooled, or mollified. She had seen it coming, and not even when she and Richard became parents in 1964—not as a matter of choice but rather on a promise to a terminally ill church officer to adopt her year-old son, Danny Jones, when she died—did it change the equation.

Unfortunately, nothing could save the marriage. While Ernestine would maintain that she and Richard had a normal sex life, she couldn't say he was a good husband, or a monogamous one; when he was busted in the bus station, she demanded no explanation but knew he was living a life separate from hers. In a broader light, the crowd he was running with was no different from the one he professed to have turned from. As she said, "I was not able to make the adjustment to Richard's way of life." And she didn't go into detail about the specific horrors, preferring late in 1963 to file for divorce on vague grounds of "extreme cruelty by the infliction of grievous mental suffering."

He put up no fight, agreeing that "I was a neglectful husband. A terrible husband." He stated that "I never loved her the way a man should love his wife," given that "I was gay and I wasn't concerned" about pleasing a wife, something he couldn't do while "I was thinking about Johnny. About Jimmy." The horny, strutting satyr of all those two-minute teen operas concluded that Ernestine "was too much woman for me. She was a whole lotta lady and I was just like a little mouse."

Quietly settling with Ernestine, he agreed to split half of his worth with her, though not any royalties, past or future, little of which he was seeing in any case. He kept the house—not a problem for her, since she would remarry in 1965—and would dutifully pay child support payments. These expenditures, too, likely played into the aim to clear a higher income. As he looked around the rock and roll map, the Beatles—who he said he had "taught to rock"—were only one of a score of acts to profit in the new market; Sam Cooke and Jackie Wilson were making bundles while Richard read his Bible. (Tragically, Cooke was killed in 1965 under mysterious circumstances at a hotel during a road tour.) And so Richard accelerated his efforts to reclaim his hard-won crown. With "Well, Alright!" still sitting on Art Rupe's shelf, and Rupe egging him to get back to work, he did, booking studio time at Los Angeles Radio Recorders studio in April 1964.

In the spirit of musical rebirth, Richard eschewed the Upsetters though he recruited not young rockers but rather Specialty veterans like producer Don Weiss and guitarists Don "Sugarcane" Harris and Dewey Terry, who had fronted the '50s doo-wop group Don and Dewey. He also hired Earl Palmer to bang on the drums for him again, but there were no horns or Billy Preston's organ. Harris and Terry were the nucleus, and they were a clued-in pair; their song "I'm Leaving It Up to You" was turned into a number one pop hit by Dale and Grace in '63 and another from 1960, "Big Boy Pete," was in '65 covered as the novelty hit "The Jolly Green Giant." (A decade later, Harris would play violin in Frank Zappa's Mothers of Invention.) They knew a good hook and how to play it, and with them Richard hoped to segue from big band to rock band, in keeping with the Beatles' template.

A third guitar man, Glenn Willings, who had a minor hit in '60 with "You Tarzan, Me Jane," also was on the session, which really was meant to get on vinyl the song both Richard and Rupe believed was his vehicle of resurrection, "Bama Lama Bama Loo." It was typically simple, inspired nonsense, a cop of "Tutti Frutti" (the lyric modified to "got a girl named Lucinder / We call her the great pretender"), the idea being to essentially transplant the traditional Little Richard lyrical and circular rhythmic formulas directly into hard rock with its electric guitar solos, which had never been prominently featured in a Little Richard record. By design and age, his voice more guttural and throaty, the title hook was punctuated by a scream repeated over and over until a full-stop ending. It rocked, all right, as did the other cuts like the Weiss composition "Poor Boy Paul" and Richard's third version of "Miss Ann."

Rupe loved them all and now ponied up the money to buy Richard out of his Atlantic contract—a thousand dollars. (Atlantic had already leased its final Richard recordings, "Milky White Way"/

"Need Him," to Coral Records, which put them out to an apathetic market late in '63). The offer Rupe gave Richard, however, was a one-shot deal continent again on proof that he indeed still had it. For Richard, it was good enough, sparing him having to spend a nickel on studio time or musicians. And, with "Bama Lama" feeling like gold in his hands—Richard pronounced it "a fantastic record"—Rupe wasted no time getting it out. Within just weeks, it was pressed and backed with Richard's "Annie is Back" (hook: "Annie's back, back, back in a brand-new Cadillac"). Sinking all he had into promoting the record and feeding the Little Richard revival story to the media and radio stations, by the late spring "Bama Loo" had made some real noise, rising to number eighty-eight both on the R&B and pop charts, number twenty in Britain. Nothing to brag about, but Richard believed he had proved he could compete in the '60s rock market, additional proof being Otis Redding's "Bama Loo" cover, "Shout Bamalama."

Richard had his own explanation—or excuse—for not charting higher. The villain, he said, was an all-powerful, conspiratorial music "establishment" that "wouldn't let [the record] through because they were afraid that I might below the whole thing open again," apparently meaning he was still too dangerous on some level. In the '50s, he said, they couldn't stop him. But, now, "they had gotten organized," not venturing who "they" were. The result of the plot, he said, "was devastating to me" and caused him to alter his perspectives. He poured his energies into the road shows, where they needed a shoehorn to pack in the huge crowds, where his white audiences were.

Not that Rupe quit trying to wring profits from the brand. As late as 1970, there would be periodic Specialty records. And even a quarter-century later, when Rupe was long gone from the business, the remnants of the company would still cash in, with the copious

Specialty Sessions—yet because of his bad contracts and settlements, Little Richard himself was cut out of whatever his name could muster in profits.

RICHARD WOULD SIGN up with another label in 1964—Vee-Jay. Fresh off of making a fortune (quickly dashed) from the American rights to the early "inferior" Beatles songs, the label's new plan was to expand Richard's new/old niche. Though the label was suffering financially, losing top acts like the Four Seasons and the Beatles, the latter's releases, for a while, kept them in the game—a game the label helped establish in the '50s with smash hits by the El Dorados, the Dells, and Jerry Butler. Richard felt at home there, and he had the benefit of being able to record at regular sessions in L.A. through 1964 and into '65. However, nothing that came out would carry much weight. Indeed, recording sometimes seemed to get in the way of all the headliner gigs Bumps Blackwell booked for Little Richard, his first major tour in the summer of '64 making hyped stops at the Hollywood Bowl, L.A.'s swinging rock club the Red Velvet, and the Cow Palace in San Francisco, then at a big oldies concert at Carnegie Hall in New York emceed by the over-caffeinated, fedora-wearing deejay Murray "The K."

Don Arden had also arranged another British tour for Richard that would have a grand finale at the Paris Olympia, sharing the stage with Chuck Berry and the Animals. And in another exceptional move, Richard made his initial appearance on *American Bandstand* in August 1964, likely the first time most of America had seen him in seven years. Viewers who had grown into maturity must have done a double take when Dick Clark introduced him and Little Richard was standing over a piano, wrapped tightly in a neat

Beatles-style suit, with short hair and no makeup as he warbled "Bama Lama Bama Loo"—notably, singing it live, not with the routine *Bandstand* lip-syncing. Seeming almost shy, he chatted with Clark, mentioning coyly that the Beatles were his warm-up act and that he had "given them their start." So ensconced, he made the rounds of the prime-time TV rock-oriented shows, such as *Shindig* and *Hollywood a Go Go*, and while in England, the counterparts *Top of the Pops* and *Ready, Steady, Go!*

Hits or not, he was of such stature that he soon became a magnet for a certain guitar player named James Marshall Hendrix. Known by few, Hendrix entered the dizzy, daffy world of Little Richard in the fall of '64 as a member of the shifting crew of sometime Upsetters and new blood that included Glenn Willings and Melvin Sparks on guitar and Johnny Franklin on bass. Ten years Richard's junior, Hendrix had been playing on the chitlin' circuit for a year after an Army hitch that had been his sentence for stealing cars in his native Seattle. After latching on with several bands and developing memorable flourishes such as playing his guitar with his teeth (which came about when a patron with a gun demanded he do so or be shot on the spot), he backed Sam Cooke, Jackie Wilson, Ike and Tina Turner, and the Isley Brothers. Backing a lower-level soul man, Gorgeous George, who took his name and wild stage garb from the '50s wrestler, Hendrix was in Atlanta when Richard came to town in November.

Richard knew nothing of the thin, wiry young man except that Gorgeous George, who Richard knew well, toured with the guitarist, and when Richard learned that Hendrix had said he would "eat ten yards of shit to join his band," the flattered Richard hired him. A strange bird, Hendrix was monstrously talented but so poor that he played a beat-up old six-string Fender Jazzmaster, with one string missing, strumming upside down because he was left-handed. He couldn't read music but what came out was otherworldly, unleashing a geyser of rhythm he could juice with fuzz, feedback, distortion, and a yowling wah-wah-pedal. Yet off stage he was eerily quiet, saying little and almost nothing in the intimidating presence of his idol.

Given the timing of Hendrix's hiring, the many claims in future years that he was on Richard's earliest recordings for Vee-Jay (including in Richard's authorized biography) are bunk—the first Vee-Jay recording took place in June 1964. However, the mystery of which songs Hendrix can be heard on was deepened by Vee-Jay's poorly documented sessions, which did identify musicians such as Terry, Harris, Willings, drummer Wade Jackson, and sax men Boogie Daniels and Frank McCray. While it has been noted that Hendrix at the time went by the pseudonym Maurice James—which is how Richard knew him—neither can that name can be found on the session sheets.

That first 1964 Vee-Jay studio date saw six tracks cut, mostly covers of '50s classics—"Hound Dog," "Blueberry Hill," "Only You," "Money Honey," and "Lawdy Miss Clawdy"—and Richard's second version of "Whole Lotta Shakin' Goin' On," as well as souped-up takes on the evergreens "Goodnight Irene" and "Memories Are Made of This." There was also "Groovy Little Suzy," a '50s-style rocker written by John Marascalco and a budding, Brooklyn-born singer-songwriter, Harry Nilsson, who sang it for Richard and was told, "My! You sing *good* for a white boy." Dedicated musicologists looking for Hendrix clues in these tracks have come up empty, as John Long's arrangements were mainly Motown-oriented, horn-driven fare with girl-group-style background harmonies. And while there would be two more sessions in 1964, it is likely that Hendrix did not participate in any Little Richard recordings until follow-up sessions for Vee-Jay in early 1965.

In truth, not even a Jimi Hendrix could have done much to elevate the tepid quality of the songs that went on the first Little Richard album for the label, *Little Richard Is Back (And There's a Whole Lotta Shakin' Goin' On!)* in the fall. Following the care and exuberance of the Specialty album, the work seemed trivial rather than moving the needle on Little Richard's comeback. It did not chart at all.

Not by coincidence, Vee-Jay was in no position to promote any of its artists. For years, its owner, Ewart Abner, had been a big spender, at least when his gambling habit paid off; at times, he took the company's payroll to Las Vegas and let it ride on a hard eight. Abner also blew tons of money on the sort of promotion methods common in the industry, such as setting up disc jockeys with prostitutes.

Richard was always impressed with how often even middling Vee-Jay records got played. But when the money ran out, so did the hits. And Richard made his recordings as the label was starting to drown. So even as Richard was being booked heavily for personal appearances, the album went nowhere. Only his residual brand carried "Whole Lotta Shakin' Goin' On," to a near top-40 placing on the R&B chart, 126 on the pop, and the B-side, "Goodnight Irene," to just 128 on the pop. That might have been a propitious start, but the subsequent singles, "Blueberry Hill"/"Cherry Hill," had no chance.

That failure was a game-changer for Richard. Vee-Jay's woes aside, he realized that he would exist on the far edges of contemporary rock, and thus wisely determined that he had no reason to musically reinvent himself; that he was a permanent delegate of rock's heritage, and that was plenty good enough. The only option was to throw all his energies into touring, where he made his money anyway, though he needed to update the act, coating it with a sheen of mod currency. He would call his band by the hip moniker of the

Crown Jewels, another reach into the British Invasion barrel. Gone now was the conservative accountant look. He grew out his hair into a wild lion's mane and began wearing flare-bottom pants and floppy hats with a feather jutting from the brim.

Invoking his new sartorial splendor, Richard dressed himself like a Carnaby Street hipster on acid, in all-too anatomically obvious pinstriped slacks, ruffled shirts with high collars, buttons undone to the navel, and high-heeled Tyrolean boots. This only applied to himself, not the band, who had to keep on dressing in conservative suits and wearing their hair short. It made for a weird contrast. The band would be escorted onto the stage by hired hands identified as His Royal Company, clad in red Buckingham Palace uniforms, tunics, and bearskin headdresses. With go-girl girls or a belly dancer gyrating, Richard would then be carried onto the darkened stage, borne on a throne in his blinding attire, illuminated by a spotlight. He was an eyeful, then an earful, just as in the old days but hip to the change all around while still steeped in the spirit of old-time rock and roll. Immune to the usual betrayals of aging—his head an unlined big, beautiful, mustached pumpkin—Little Richard in his early thirties had discovered a fountain of youth. Now if only he could keep himself from drowning in it.

HE WAS UNDENIABLY a legend, and a still shining one. You could not pick out anyone who came of age as a rock and roller in the '50s who wasn't influenced by him in some way, directly or indirectly. One example was Ike and Tina Turner. Of course, Ike had greatly influenced Richard with the shuffling piano beat of "Rocket 88," but in the mid-'60s the Ike and Tina Revue seemed a victim of the British Invasion; they could get few bookings until they signed with

Loma Records and released two electrifying live albums produced by Bumps Blackwell, who connected them with Richard. And Ike, as had James Brown, learned that even a cursory conversation with Little Richard could be worth a fortune. Richard got up and showed Tina a few steps she could use and offered some vocal advice. As a result, Ike recalled, "I'd be writing songs with Little Richard in mind [and] Tina was my Little Richard. Listen closely to Tina and who do you hear? Little Richard singing in a female voice."

By decade's end, the Ike and Tina Revue was one of the world's top attractions.

Meanwhile, the world's top attraction was still in thrall to Richard. Even though they were light years beyond any other act in show business, the Beatles would recede in his company; when they toured the West Coast, they would stay not in a ritzy hotel but at his house.

But Richard's own winding road back to the devil's music caused static in his own backyard. Not only did the Seventh-day Adventists feel betrayed, but pastors at individual black churches, especially in the South, tried to keep him from performing at the soul clubs in their areas. Because of the backlash, some gigs were canceled, and sales of his records stagnated among the black buying public.

For even loyal Richard fans, who couldn't get with the thrones, silver wigs, and spangled, gold lamé jackets, he seemed engaged not in an evolution but self-parody.

Because his England tours were never shy of fans, he actually put on a toned-down show there. But in his own country he figured he needed the extra dazzle. Trouble was, it didn't work everywhere. The South was a problem beyond the hectoring preachers. There, glitz and Vegas-style overkill turned off many who had come to see him as he was when he was a "dangerous" black man, not a negative image of white rock and roll tastes. And white audiences weren't particularly aware of Liberace anymore, though he would constantly refer to himself as the black version of Liberace.

To various segments of the population, he was a has-been, and at times he played before a handful of people. It seemed he couldn't win. His long-again hair, which had once been part of his persona, was in the politicized culture of the '60s prone to making him a "long-haired hippie freak" to some. The notion that Little Richard had to deal with a backlash in 1965 seems absurd. But as he saw it, stinging backlash was responsible for TV producers keeping him off the variety shows. Richard's exile had cost him, in his estimation, millions of dollars. But he didn't expect that his return to prominence still would cost him. Something always did, it seemed.

What saved him was his catalog of priceless songs, which seemed to have a life all their own, enveloping and preserving him through troubling times. As it was, he felt the pressure to keep his touring profitable, but because that was problematic, his personal relationships with his band began to seriously erode. And that wrote an end to the glorified overlap of history of Little Richard and Jimi Hendrix.

With Hendrix in the band, more Vee-Jay sessions were held in December 1964, with Richard updating many of his familiar oldies in a Motownish vein with a horn section and a four-four beat. There would then be at least three more recording dates early in '65, when it was all too clear that Richard's voice was no longer able to hit the high notes or shrieks without audible straining, though he could get away with positioning himself as a more mature Little Richard.

Still, in keeping with his lowered expectations for making records, his studio output was haphazard and chaotic. Some sessions were in L.A., others in New York with jazz producer Joe Fields, others perhaps Chicago, Vee-Jay's home base, judging by the next Little Richard single, "Cross Over"/"It Ain't Watcha Do (It's The

Way How You Do It)," a rip of the old jazz song "Tain't What You Do (It's the Way That You Do It)," the first written by Richard's sometimes sax player Red Tyler, the second by Richard and jazz trumpeter Ray Codrington, and produced, respectively, by Chicago mainstays Richard Parker and Calvin Carter, who had founded Vee-Jay with his sister and brother-in-law.

Released early in 1965 even though they weren't on the next Little Richard album, the misleadingly titled *Little Richard's Greatest Hits* (more accurate would have been "Little Richard's new versions of Little Richard's greatest hits"), they were notably better than the album fodder, with Richard abandoning his usual breakneck pace and high-pitched yowling for more melodic, bluesy intonations. And while it is not certain that Hendrix was in the house for these tracks, "It Ain't Whatcha Do," with its crisp, nuanced electric guitar riffs, makes speculation obvious. Still, neither song charted. With Vee-Jay on its last legs, the label raced to get the most out of its Little Richard product, of which there may have been as many as fifty tracks in the bank.

The next, released as a single in June, was "Without Love," Clyde McPhatter's 1957 soul hit. Also covered by Elvis, it was an emotionally wrought, gospel-rendered love plea swathed by layers of strings and a chorale. Backed with "Dance What You Wanna," it flopped, as did a single in October as two parts of the same song, Don Covay's languid blues ballad about sticking it out with a cheating lover, "I Don't Know What You've Got (But It's Got Me)," again produced by Calvin Carter. Despite getting no traction, it is this blues-busting song, in which Richard knotted up in another gospel barrage and injected a proto-rap referring to himself in the third person, that would attract much notice in succeeding years as having included not only Jimi Hendrix but also Billy Preston on organ and Covay on backing vocals. Hendrix's bluesy, stabbing electric guitar riffs that opened the song and goosed it all the way through is indeed a signature of his style, which can be found in a smattering of other Vee-Jay recordings; by some accounts, he played on at least fourteen sessions with Richard, none with the stamp of "I Don't Know."

Whatever the count of such collaborations, these were the only examples of Little Richard and Jimi Hendrix making beautiful music together in the studio (only one grainy home movie of a live performance of Hendrix in the band during a TV show seems to exist). As it turned out, they were little more than two ships passing in the night, and for both it was a hell of a ride.

ten

DO WHATEVER YOU FEEL

Bad pay, lousy living, and getting burned.   **—JIMI HENDRIX**
on his time in Little Richard's band

Vee-Jay Records, $3 million in the hole in 1965 and soon to declare bankruptcy, had begun pawning off its remaining Little Richard product, including piles of studio tracks and tapes of numerous live performances. Some of the tapes were complete songs, some not, some extended versions of the oldies, some raw demos, some outtakes. Albums carved from these remnants would appear for years on various labels. As for Richard himself, his next landing spot was Modern Records, which seemed like a natural move, as the label had an enviable history as an influential player in big band and R&B music. In the '50s, it was home to Etta James, Ike and Tina Turner, Howlin' Wolf, and John Lee Hooker, then when it began to go broke it ceased operations in 1958 and six years later revived in a last-ditch attempt to stay solvent. In fact, Little Richard would be one of its last star names, though it invested very little in him and got even less in return, as recording was now of secondary importance to touring, something that became absolutely necessary when by the new year of 1966 Richard had not been in the studio for Modern at all.

Instead, he was on the road endlessly, keeping a killing schedule, the strains of which caused Jimi Hendrix in particular to become disgruntled—ironically, as the result of Richard's advice to him not to be "ashamed to do whatever you feel" because "the people can tell if you're phony." Taking it to heart, Hendrix began grousing, mostly about money issues, later claiming that Richard owed him back pay amounting to a thousand dollars.

The partnership was both exhilarating and thorny, and while historical revisionists have carved out the facile narrative that Richard in time could not abide the fact that Hendrix increasingly drew too much of the attention and oxygen to himself, it's not as facile as that. He dug Jimi to no end, allowing him to steal a song with an unplanned solo during which he would play with his teeth or behind his head. Richard even turned-on the famed R&B blues guitarist Albert Collins to Hendrix, having them jam together. Indeed, Jimi would say that Richard helped bring him out of his shell, and Richard had never seen anyone, other than himself, who could generate the gape-jawed amazement by creating what Jimi would codify later in song and by pouring lighter fluid on his guitar (literally stealing his fire, the one Richard lit years before when he set his piano to flames). Ever the narcissist, Richard was flattered when Jimi took to wearing a headband under his bushy hairline after Richard started wearing one.

While Richard wouldn't admit it, there was much about Jimi to emulate, Richard's new updated image really an imitation of the younger man's fashion and attitude. If Richard understood that he wasn't the future of rock and roll, he also could gain a great deal from a man who would be that future (if all too briefly). If Richard was nothing close to psychedelic—the brand soon defined by Jimi but played only in fleeting doses in Richard's backup band—Richard relished being the mentor of a guitar player like Hendrix, provided the guitar player accepted that he would never be the star of the show. There was only one of those, one boss, with the assumption of privilege.

And Richard, for his part, laid all the blame for the falling out on "Maurice," who flouted Richard's rule against moonlighting with other bands, missing bus rides, drinking before a show and smoking a cigarette on stage, and sometimes sloppy guitar work that would make Richard grit his teeth. At one gig, at the Royal Peacock in Atlanta, when Jimi was into one of his long solos, Richard was so livid that he yelled, "Stop the music!" and started the song over, not allowing the solo this time. At other times, Richard bridled when Jimi and the band's other guitar player, Glenn Willings, decided to discard the black suits and wear colorful shirts. Hendrix would later recreate Richard's high-pitched, squeaky bellowing at a hastily called band meeting.

"Hendrix, you be deaf?" he told him, "You get rid of that shirt, boy! I am Little Richard, and I am the King of Rock and Rhythm, and I am the one who's going to look pretty on stage."

Richard went further when Jimi again broke the dress code, raging at him, "Shit . . . you fired!" But he recanted when Hendrix sold the loud shirt the next day. At another meeting, Richard lit into the young man for his wild hair, even though Richard had let his own mane grow long after seeing Jimi do so. As Hendrix recalled, "I said I wasn't going to cut my hair for anybody." That cost him another five bucks, and the fear of such indiscriminate fines chilled the entire band, all of whom, Jimi said, were "brainwashed." One of them, Buddy Travis, said that Richard "would fine us fifty dollars if we didn't call him 'King.' He even fined [another band mate] for smiling during a performance. [We] were supposed to stand there without any expression," only cementing the slight that they lived with, as mere courtiers, never to steal any of Little Richard's wattage.

AS MUCH AS a martinet as Richard was, Jimi was surely getting a priceless, if difficult, education. His manner of dress was a direct reflection of how cool he thought Richard was; in time, all of Hendrix's trademarks—his hair, his headbands, and the Old West gambler hats with a feather sticking from them—were taken from Little Richard. But for all the positive synergy they had, too much static drove them apart. As it was, Hendrix was working for him one tour at a time, not knowing after each if he was still in the band until Richard would hire him for the next. And Richard, despite claiming Hendrix as his exclusive property, believed the informality of it all was cause to withhold as much money from him as he deemed proper. Buddy Travis, too, was shorted by Richard; owed $400, he recalled, "I grabbed a wire coat hanger, and I was going to stab Richard if he didn't pay us our money."

Of his time with Richard, Jimi would say, "It was okay at first, but then you get to a point when you can't stand anymore." His precis of it all—"Bad pay, lousy living, and getting burned"—was a short version of an existence in which things could get out of control very fast. At the late April string of shows at the Paramount in New York, promoter Morris Levy, the Mob-connected owner of Roulette Records and the Birdland jazz club (who would later be convicted of extortion), told Richard he had to cut his set to a stifling ten minutes. Mortally offended, he announced to the crowd, "Management doesn't want me to play any more music. How do you feel about that?," prompting a cascade of boos.

Richard kept singing until the curtain was dropped on him, then, with Hendrix, headed for Levy's temporary backstage office as the crowd began a near riot and police were called in. Pushing Levy's door open, Richard showered the wise guy with profanities and Levy leaped out of his chair. Any more lip, he hissed, and "You'll find yourself floating in a lake," no idle threat coming from him. They were also confronted in an elevator by a stage manager who told Richard he'd never play the theater again. Among those witnessing this was Eric Burdon of the Animals, who were in the house.

"Richard exploded," he said. "With his high-pitched voice, he sounded like an old woman gone berserk. The young black kid trying to hold him back was Hendrix."

Clamped in a headlock by a cop, Richard screamed maniacally, "Those little white girls out there love me!" He went on kicking and screaming even as the cop was holding a gun to his head, at one point warning him, "If you don't shut up, I'm going to blow your head off."

As Fate would have it, that night was when Hendrix met the Animals' bass player, Chas Chandler, who would become his manager and overseer of his meteoric but short-lived rise to the penthouse of rock. But he hung on with Richard a while longer, and when the session in New York at which "I Don't Know What You've Got (But It's Got Me)" was recorded, Jimi found himself viewed as something like Richard's bodyguard. The headliner of that Paramount show, the after-school TV comedian Soupy Sales, who had a novelty hit out, "Do the Mouse," swore for years that Richard blamed him for cutting down his set and vowed to "get" Soupy, who went on stage that night terrified he would be gunned down by a "hit man," presumably meaning the scowling Hendrix.

Jimi could put up with a lot, but things got just too wavy when Richard apparently made him a target of his hormonal urges. Years later, Hendrix's girlfriend Rosa Brooks went on record saying that, after a year, Hendrix "was under so much stress from being chased by Little Richard" that he was "ready to get away from him." Hendrix, who wasn't only straight but apparently homophobic—he would privately imitate Richard in a fey voice and call him "Little Bitchard" or the "Queen of Rock and Roll" (not that this would have offended Richard, who called himself such at times)—fended him off, whereupon Richard had another suggestion. Said Brooks: "Jimi told me that Richard wanted to see us make out and stuff, but I was never into any of that."

Things were clearly going downhill, their kinship frayed. Richard now believed Hendrix's solos were intentionally long, making Little Richard seem like a mere sideman sometimes. But money was the tipping point. Richard's elaborate shows were costing him as much as making him. Having to put up around $16,000 of his own money to finance one tour that lasted until almost the end of the year, he had even less reason to compensate Hendrix and the other band guys. Usually when his guys henpecked him about it, Richard would pay up, prodded by his brother Robert, who had the impossible job of road manager, but the end result would be Richard spitefully firing the guy. And that ending awaited Hendrix, who got his money during the '65 summer tour but, despite having shielded Richard during the Paramount kerfuffle a month and a half before, was marked for execution. His last appearance with the band came in early June at a week-long engagement at the Apollo Theater. Then, when the troupe boarded the bus for the next gig in Washington, D.C., Jimi missed it. They didn't wait for him. Hours later, when Hendrix called Robert, he was canned.

Robert would, implausibly, claim the decision was made solely by him, not Richard. "I fired Hendrix," he said, not for demanding money or resisting sexual advances. "He was a damn good guitar player, but the guy was never on time. He was always late for the bus and flirting with the girls and stuff like that. [So] I finally got Richard to cut him loose. We had some words. I explained [that] I was running the road for Richard and I didn't accept that kind of bullshit."

And so they parted ways, one an icon in perpetuity, the other an icon to be—though when he was cast adrift, Hendrix, even with the back pay, was so down and out that he had to pawn his guitar for sixty dollars and eat tomato paste as meals. Neither spoke of Richard's alleged pursuit of Jimi as an object of affection, perhaps the only such matter Richard would ever avoid talking about, and in fact the two would regularly chat on the phone. Their mutual encomiums as cosmic music forces were not crimped, although in a comical footnote, one of those slapdash albums of Little Richard material, released on the ALA label in 1972 after Hendrix's death, was called *Friends from the Beginning: Little Richard & Jimi Hendrix*—something they never were (and totally bogus, as Hendrix hadn't played on any of the album's tracks). Jimi also insisted he hadn't been fired at all; rather, he said, he up and quit a month later, in July. Buddy Travis backed that up, saying that Richard was "upset" when he learned Hendrix had left. And Richard simply let Robert's version be, offering no further comment.

Neither did Hendrix's link to Little Richard end. The next act he hooked with, a singer-producer-label owner named Alexander Randolph, who went by Mr. Wiggles (one of his more famous songs was "Agent 00-Soul"), was close to Richard and performed with the original Upsetters. And Richard lodged no objection to Hendrix being hired. A year later, after other numerous fleeting gigs, he was signed by Chas Chandler, who produced his first recordings in London, "Hey Joe" and "Purple Haze," and an album *Are You Experienced*, which spent 33 weeks on the charts and went double platinum. When he and The Jimi Hendrix Experience became all the rage on both sides of the Atlantic Ocean, and Paul McCartney was calling Hendrix "Sgt. Pepper," it gave Richard another protege to boast about having pointed the way to illustrious fame, right down to his look. When Robert saw the name splashed all over the rock press, he asked Richard who this Jimi Hendrix fellow was.

Richard laughed. "You know who that is?" he told his brother. "That's Maurice James!"

MEANWHILE, STAYING FAMOUS was something Little Richard didn't have to fret about, though it was still more certain when he would tour England, as he often did. On one of those tours, another impressionable Brit rocker was a piano player in one of the opening acts, Bluesology. Reggie Dwight, who would soon assume the name of Elton John, recalled the vision of Little Richard "standing on top of the piano, all lights, sequins, and energy." He also recalled his band being booed off the stage by fans who were there only to see that same vision. To be sure, Richard's recording load for Modern was irregular, as the label, like Vee-Jay, had little resources for studio or promotion costs. The first work to be released was a live album of the oldies he had recorded at Atlanta's Domino Club in December 1965, produced by Bumps Blackwell who overdubbed a tepid show with embellished crowd noise to boost the live feel, adding one new tune they had cowritten, "Do You Feel It," a

Wilson Pickett-style funk chug, cleaved into two parts, to be released in February as a double-sided single.

The record, *The Incredible Little Richard Sings His Greatest Hits—Live!* hit the shelves in limited numbers just after the new year, seemingly as another trifle dropped into the pool of Little Richard repackaged albums.

It didn't make a dent on the charts. Nor did the first Modern single, also issued that month, "Holy Mackerel," a Richard composition, backed with Lloyd Price's "Baby, Don't You Want a Man Like Me." The real pity was the failure of the latter two, for which Blackwell went all in on the Stax model, going with Richard to Memphis to cut seven tracks after renting from the label's owner, Jim Stewart, the same studio on McLemore Street where Otis Redding, Sam and Dave, and Eddie Floyd brought soul to full fruition, and hiring the famed Memphis Horns to back Richard with heated flourishes. It was an historic scenario for sure, and the results were engaging, although while intending to sound like Otis, the sound of "Holy Mackerel" was pure Richard—more of a throwback, sounding much like the New Orleans sessions—the title intoned by the actor who used to say the phrase on the '50s black sitcom *Amos and Andy*. On "Baby, Don't You Want a Man Like Me," Richard's gruff vocal in a lower key than normal came off more like James Brown. But enticing as they were, the songs prefaced not a full-blown Little Richard comeback as a relevant rocker but rather only a similar letdown when, a month later, the "Do You Feel It" sides hit the market and also went nowhere.

By then, Richard's Modern contract had run out, in January 1966, and he signed another contract with Okeh Records—making for a rather confusing situation since Modern would go on putting out Richard singles as late as November 1967, with "Baby What You Want Me to Do" parts one and two. In fact, it would take until

June for the first Okeh product to be issued, only weeks before the Modern release of "Directly from My Heart"/"I'm Back" was also out, competing for the same market. Few could keep straight which records were on which labels. And Richard was increasingly sour on Okeh, yet another hoary "race record" label and a subsidiary of Columbia Records, which separated soul like the Chicago-based R&B of Major Lance from mainstream fare like Bobby Vinton and bands like the Dave Clark Five and Hollies who were released on its Epic sub-label.

That was where Richard believed he should be, having experienced the apathy shown his records in the black market. To his dismay, when he arrived at Okeh, his former Specialty label mate and imitator Larry Williams—who wound up there when he had gotten out of prison—had been tapped to produce him. Williams was now in a more hardcore R&B vein, fronting a band led by blues man Johnny "Guitar" Watson. Not at all chastened by jail, Williams had resumed his old self-destructive routines, which did not bode well for either him or Richard. Planning Richard's recording, Williams gave him little say. Larry had dug the Vee-Jay live album and became Richard's musical director for a series of dates at Okeh's Hollywood music club. But due to the poor acoustics at the club he turned Columbia's studio into a night club, filling it with people told to make a lot of noise at the first session on January 25, 1966.

Thirteen songs would go on the album, its title almost identical to the Modern album, *Little Richard's Greatest Hits—Recorded Live!* Nine were covers of his oldies, the others a cover of Jimmy Reed's "Baby What You Want Me to Do" (retitled "Any Way You Want Me"), Wilson Pickett's "Don't Fight It" (retitled "You Gotta Feel It"), and Richard's "Get Down With It (Do the Jerk)." The play-out track was an instrumental of James Brown's "The Scratch." It was meant to be cool, and it was. Besides Watson the session men were

Billy Preston and two of Richard's band, Glenn Willings and Eddie Fletcher. But to Richard it felt like *he* was doing the imitating, hemmed again into the horn-heavy Stax corner, not the colorblind Little Richard corner.

The first Little Richard single on Okeh, both sides taken from the same session, Williams and Watson's "Poor Dog (Who Can't Wag His Own Tail)" and a redo of "Well Alright," got him back on the charts, going to number forty-one on the R&B chart, 121 on the pop. And when the full album hit the shelves in July, it made some waves, too, hitting number twenty-eight on the R&B chart though barely having a pulse on the pop, at 181. Again, it seemed like a propitious start, provided follow-ups could continue the groove.

Larry Williams surely tried hard. When Richard was on another of his English tours in December, Williams booked another famous rock landmark—the EMI studio on Abbey Road, where the Beatles mostly recorded—to cut four tracks with sidemen led by Britain's top session guitarist "Big Jim" Sullivan and producer Norman "Hurricane" Smith, who had engineered every Beatles record made there until 1965.

Smith, who would have his own singing career in the '70s, remembered that Richard came in that day with a sore throat, soothing it with throat spray and liquor, but that "I've never seen an artist work so hard—or perspire as much," his voice "so clear and strong you'd never believe he had a bad throat." Two tracks, "Get Down With It"—which Smith called "a powerhouse rocker"—and "Rosemary," would be released as the A and B sides of a single but one that was only released in England in February 1967, without charting, another letdown for Richard. Of more urgency for his label was the release a month before of *The Explosive Little Richard* album, with Williams producing and again ignoring Richard's input, leaning even more on the Stax and Motown formulas of fat-bottom rhythm, bone-shaking brass, and the new trend of synthesized keyboards emulating strings. Culled from several studio sessions, there were no updates of Richard's oldies—and no songs at all from Richard's pen while there were three ("Poor Dog," "The Commandments of Love," "I Need Love") from Williams's. The eclectic mix also drew from inspired sources: Berry Gordy's "Do You Love Me," Chris Kenner's "Land of a Thousand Dances," Chuck Willis's "Don't Deceive Me (Please Don't Go)," the Holland-Dozier-Holland "Function at the Junction," and the Sam Cooke "Well Alright."

These numbers surely had the feel of a square peg being jammed into a round hole, even if Richard was versatile enough to make the material work with his amazing vocal range and depth. Not that he was seen as a top-shelf contemporary act, but his unchallenged role as the keeper of original rock's eternal flame was not disturbed by his admirable attempt to evolve. In the new *Rolling Stone*, which debuted that year, the album was given a "favorable" rating, which was like a huzzah for a journal that got off on being acrid. In the more effusive *Crawdaddy*, begun the year before, reviewer Jim Payne called it a "solid album" and opined, "The amazing thing is that when you start listening to some of the stuff he was doing in the early '50s you find out that it's really a very contemporary sound." Though he quibbled that "The result is Little Richard in several contemporary R&B bags but without the distinctive Little Richard quality that would have made the album a real success. A fine rendering of a broad idiom but lacking the individual style to make it truly creative."

Across the pond, *Melody Maker* wrote of "I Need Love," with a touch of Brit snark, "Umm. Oh yeah, it's Little Richard. Doesn't that guy work hard. It's a strong tune all right. Just before that solo thing though he loses fire and let's [*sic*] the whole thing slide down. Oh. He's picked it right back up again." Still, these sort of encomiums, even backhanded ones, were catnip for Richard, convincing him he was back in the game. Particularly salient was Payne's sage observation that "I Need Love," "The Commandments of Love," and "Money" were "very James Brown influenced," the irony being that "James Brown was probably influenced by Little Richard himself." But the promise of "Poor Dog" was false; the next single, "I Need Love," went nowhere. Neither did the later release of the itchy dance stomp "(You're My Girl) I Don't Want to Discuss It" and two more singles in March and June 1968 (though "Discuss It" would have a second life in '70s rock, covered by Delaney & Bonnie & Friends, with a guitar solo by Eric Clapton, and becoming a standard in their live set list).

In the wake of the failure to lift off in sales and on the charts, Richard steamed, concluding it was the fault of anyone but himself. And the main villain was Williams, who he took to savaging in interviews, calling him "the worst producer in the world," who drowned his vocals with trumpets, adding, "He wanted me to copy Motown and I'm no Motown artist. I got so I wanted to throw all the trumpets in the world into the river. He wants me to do all that electronics and stuff; I want the natural real thing, the real people want the real thing. He's a very bad producer, very bad. In fact, he's one of the worst I've seen." He also trashed Okeh for not recording him on the Epic label where he could be better positioned for white audiences. Still believing he could achieve rebirth as a hit-maker if only he could get the proper support—and if he could record for a label that wasn't about to die—he left Okeh for the next company waiting with outstretched arms and a contract, Brunswick Records.

But he would not stray too far from the man he was reviling, who would for years have a whole different role in his life—

supplying him with all manner of drugs. For now, it was mainly weed, but he had already expanded to experimenting with the hard stuff, heroin and cocaine, and his open boozing meant that his tee-total days were over. He seemed to need more and more of these feel-good salves as he backslid into the feckless, sybaritic ways—which included the all-night orgies and "pumping." If all this was an indication that he wanted to self-medicate as a way of insulating himself from the disappointment of his records, it also meant that Larry Williams would be a constant in his life for some time to come, which would very nearly kill him.

BRUNSWICK SEEMED A good fit for Little Richard. Once the home of Al Jolson and Bing Crosby and race-record kings like Cab Calloway, Duke Ellington, and Fletcher Henderson, it too went under and then revived as a property of Decca Records. In the '50s it entered the rock era with stars like Buddy Holly and Jackie Wilson, and it would be a soul music leader into the '70s. What's more, the half-dozen or so songs recorded by Richard for the label were produced by no less than Nat Tarnopol, Jackie Wilson's former manager and Brunswick's executive vice-president, one of the industry's most important power brokers. He backed Richard with the Bert Decoteaux Orchestra and its chorale, and four singles were cut in the label's New York studio, two coming out late in '67, two more in the spring and summer of '68. The most intriguing was Don Covay's "Soul Train," a boogaloo funk of syncopated, scratchy guitars, rumbling basses, and blaring horns, a vibrant presaging of disco and the '70s TV dance party for black teens with the same name. This was the niche Tarnopol saw for Richard, given his infectious stomping and squealing. Same with another Covay number, the laid-back "Try Some of Mine," the change of pace being the sweaty throwback blues of Lightnin' Hopkins's "Baby Don't You Tear My Clothes."

However, none of the records were even low-level hits on any chart, and Richard nursed his fixed grudge about not being positioned to the white market. Exercising his option, he walked again, leaving a live album titled *Little Richard Sings At The Aladdin* to be shelved, never to be heard. (Unlike the previous labels he had left, Brunswick would not post-release or repackage its Little Richard stock.) Leaving when he did was good and bad. The bad: not being there when the label hit the jackpot in the '70s' disco/smooth soul era. But the good was that he avoided being caught up in Tarnopol's descent, which saw him charged with tax fraud and payola charges. Tarnopol beat the charges, but the company went broke. Its artists were left out in the cold, and in the '80s Brunswick folded into corporate mergers. Just another squalid rock and roll parable, the kind that Richard lived with his entire career. He had known crooks and liars, and he had harbored the cynical conclusion that everyone in the business was one or the other, or both.

It would be another two years before he hooked up with another label, gaining far more satisfaction on the road, where he was raking in some high-end paydays for regular gigs in Vegas. But the lack of enough liquid assets always seemed to be an issue. Given his irregular schedule, at times taking on a gig at the last minute, he often had to travel to destinations without a band and hire musicians on the fly. For these expenses he had to call Bumps Blackwell, who would keep a reserve of funds set aside by Richard to be able to cover expense checks. Bumps had done well ushering Richard onto TV shows, as well, such as Pat Boone's variety series.

But he and Blackwell had never really sealed their divisions. For one thing, Richard could never understand why Blackwell had made Sam Cooke a fortune while Richard was always a step from being a pauper. Cooke, a rarity for any artist but especially black artists of the time, owned his own publishing rights and his own studio. Not only had Bumps never shared those objectives for Richard, Blackwell was skimming from the top, Richard believed, later saying Bumps was "enjoying the money I was making," and that he would "get nasty and shout at me. . . . So I fired him." He did so on a whim, with no regard to the fact that Bumps had him under contract. (Blackwell maintained he didn't sue because it would have left Richard penniless.) Richard then hired Sam Cooke's main man from the old days, J.W. Alexander. But that only lasted a few months before Richard felt J.W. was spending too much time with his main client, Lou Rawls, and not enough on him. And so Richard fired J.W. and rehired none other than Bumps Blackwell—for a third time.

IF ALL THIS seemed like a chaotic way to conduct his career, to those who knew him it was classic Little Richard, a man who had never lived any other way. The difference was that he had to accept living a less-than-large life now. The royalties from the many records he had made were minimal, the advances gone, and studio expenses deducted from his proceeds. Resistant to crimp his old habit of spending what he had lavishly, by the late '60s he was just about bankrupt. To free up funds he sold his castle and moved to a less affluent neighborhood in Riverside called Larchmont Village, sharing the new home with Leva Mae and her husband; for his siblings he rented small apartments. Rarely was he around the family, however. Instead, he held his place on the periphery of rock, performing up to 200 gigs a year, blissfully separated from the revolving trends in music that seemed to rise with the latest Beatles album. In '67, *Sgt. Pepper* sparked the "Summer of Love," with people walking around with flowers in their hair and acid under their tongues, ringing in the era of acid rock.

As the crazy war in the Asian jungle kept escalating, scars were left everywhere in America, and it seemed Little Richard was an antidote, chasing away turmoil and trepidation by reviving all of their past lives when things were so carefree, or felt like they had been. He was no counter-culture icon, nor was he ever, but few knew how to define him anymore while many Baby Boomers were losing their rebelliousness, becoming wealthy and conventional— and, as crazy as it seemed, this was now a target audience for him, explaining why he was headlining not on the soul circuit but at glittery weeklong runs in Las Vegas. He was dismissed by some as an artifact, yet he was more relevant than his failed records would have indicated.

If not a trend-setter, he was set into stone as something just as good—a creature comfort. He was booked into highly paid appearances at L.A.'s hip hot spots like Ciro's, the Whisky a Go Go, the Red Velvet, and the Hollywood Palladium, and Bill Graham's Fillmore Auditorium in San Francisco, where he proved he could still sell out a major hall as effortlessly as could Jefferson Airplane and the Grateful Dead. In between, he could leap onto the lucrative oldies circuit or something like the Allentown State Fair.

While he could fit seamlessly into acid rock's chemically altered verbal images of funeral pyres and apocalyptic doom, it mattered not that he was nothing like "hip" in the sense of a Hendrix or the former gospel-singing Chambers Brothers, who sang of being "psychedelicized." It wasn't just that his own drug use was kept strictly on the down-low. Now, *not* being aimed at a hardcore black market was actually beneficial; it allowed him to hover on the periphery of rock, ready to jump in and lighten the mood, "Tutti Frutti" a battle cry and means of escapism with magical restorative powers of wonderfully misbegotten youth. To be sure, many of his contemporary warhorses were also being given their well-earned due by the rock intelligentsia that had been bred on their music. But only Little Richard could demand top billing and top money, even if he could never seem to keep much of it in his pocket.

eleven

SNATCHED FROM THE BURNING

[M]usic works in a cycle. Where else can it go? It's just a tall building but it has a foundation; if you take the foundation out the top is gonna fall. This music is the true foundation of the music, what they're doing today all stems from this. So the kids are going back to it, they heard their mothers talking and they want to get a chance to see what their mothers really enjoyed, and they're gonna enjoy what their mothers didn't get a chance to enjoy. **—LITTLE RICHARD,** 1970

*I*f rock and roll were here to stay, so too was Little Richard. As the '60s wound on, shooting from one trend to another, he was an oddity, an effeminate xerox of Jimi Hendrix with the distinguishing element of camp, shtick, dripping with history. His hair was piled-up and curled, his garb skintight pants and navel-cut tops with crystal mini-mirrors. In rock and roll, everything old is recycled as new and so the look seemed not even garish but rather a souped-up version of himself, not an agent of change but a timeless rock and roll traveler. Not really needing to pander to current rock formats, *he* provided the context, of the rebel spirit of rock that would never die. He was cemented to the origins of rock and himself as its avatar, able to preach the word of God while wearing Spandex and in between songs about getting some in the back seat.

A British rock paper critic, as had forbears a decade before, wrote of Little Richard causing mayhem on the stage, reporting how a "motley of drape-jacketed rockers were jiving on stage and bowing down at [Richard's] feet before being thrown back from whence they came . . . . [T]he stalls swayed in one continuous mass of rockin', stompin', hypnotised humanity and finishing with a more cohesive 'Whole Lotta Shakin', Richard left the stage, every nervous inch of his brown frame bathed in perspiration."

The best way to analyze why he remained so popular, then, was to not even try. It was a lot easier to just go watch him weave his spell, never adjusting his set list. In 1968, a balm for the unending line of convulsive events in the real world, he tore up the Schaefer Music Festival in New York's Central Park, sharing the bill with the Chambers Brothers, and closed out the year at the Aladdin Hotel in Reno, breaking Sammy Davis Jr.'s attendance records there. Then, in '69—the year the Beatles split up, men walked on the moon, and half a million strong assembled for a music festival on a farm in Woodstock—Little Richard was inexplicably part of the narrative. He began the year with a sentimental journey back to the Star-Club in Hamburg and then made stops in Switzerland and Canada, the latter stop in one of that country's earliest mass open-air rock concerts, the 12-hour Toronto Rock and Roll Revival, on May 7.

Its roll call of acts was a virtual who's who of two generations at least, from Little Richard, Bo Diddley, Jerry Lee Lewis, Gene

Vincent, and Chuck Berry to the Doors and the then-Chicago Transit Authority and Alice Cooper (who made his name at this event by infamously biting the head off a chicken)—though it became something more historic when John Lennon agreed at the last minute to participate to promote the first iteration of the Plastic Ono Band, with Yoko, Klaus Voormann, Alan White, and Eric Clapton. Lennon, who a week later would officially quit the Beatles, agreed to be paid nothing in exchange for first-class tickets from England and hotel suites and a supply of cocaine for his troupe while in Toronto—but when Richard got wind that promoter Johnny Brower was paying the Doors $25,000, he demanded the same, and received it, though John would be the closer.

Richard had earned the privilege to earn that much and he ran with it, garnering a crowd reaction that far surpassed those to both Jim Morrison and Lennon's blitzed-out, ragged performances before 25,000 packed into a stadium at the University of Toronto, one review reporting that "he and his extremely tight band proceeded to tear through his classics at breakneck speed. With sweat gushing down his heavily made up face, he jumped on the piano and drove the young crowd crazy, exhorting them to get up and dance . . . . By the time he finished [he] was sopping wet with his shirt torn to shreds by the crowd below."

Though he'd been out of exile for seven years, the review concluded that "In thirty frenetic minutes Little Richard had just made his comeback." And clearly, when Lennon heard and felt the place shaking, he knew he had walked into a garden rake having to follow Little Richard—a task no sane human would want—and unveil his new band. As he would recall, "I threw up for hours before I went on. I could hardly sing any of the numbers. I was full of shit." The crowd was brutal, booing lustily as he sang songs contrived on the spot as Yoko did her ear-punishing "vocals" and the guitars squawked in deafening feedback. With no recourse, they all walked off the stage, the booing becoming like a hailstorm.

While Morrison had graciously paid tribute to the "illustrious musical geniuses" of the past, Lennon would ignore everyone else when he released in December the debut Plastic Ono Band album *Live Peace in Toronto 1969*, smartly overdubbing and cleaning the tracks of the booing and Yoko's parts. Similarly, on the DVD *John Lennon and the Plastic Ono Band: Live in Toronto*, eight tracks by his band dwarfed the one each by Richard ("Lucille"), Berry, Lewis, and Diddley, the others stiffed altogether. (Better late than never, the full set by Richard came out in 2003 as the must-have DVD *Little Richard: Live at the Toronto Peace Festival*.) But if Lennon had the turf to himself, Toronto was the best evidence yet that Little Richard could still play in the rock and roll sandbox.

BY SUMMER, HE had burnished his legend's credentials, appearing with Fats Domino and Jerry Lee Lewis as guests on the Monkees' TV special, *33⅓ Revolutions Per Monkee*, in which Richard in one segment danced on his piano bench and in another was part of an amazing optical illusion as the three legends played pianos stacked one on top of the other. There were also guest shots on Della Reese's TV show, then on Tom Jones's. Meanwhile, the endless road led him to the hip New York clubs Ungano's and the Fillmore East. Even sans new hits, the shows were sellouts, and led up to another rock milestone of the era, the Atlantic City Pop Festival on August 1–3, 1969.

Held at the Atlantic City Racetrack in Mays Landing, New Jersey, it was quickly lost in the shadow of Woodstock, which occurred only twelve days after, but was temporarily the first major outdoor music fest on the East Coast. The list of acts was nearly as star-studded, with several acts playing both. For a then-pricey fifteen-dollar top ticket for all three days, 100,000 each day stood in oppressive heat and rain, most too stoned to know they were being rained on. The marquee was awesome—the first day included Joni Mitchell, Iron Butterfly, Procol Harum, Santana, Chambers Brothers, Booker T. and the M.G.'s, and Chicago; the second, Jefferson Airplane, Creedence Clearwater Revival, B.B. King, the Byrds, and the Butterfield Blues Band; the third, Janis Joplin, Canned Heat, Mothers of Invention, Sir Douglas Quintet, Dr. John, Joe Cocker, Three Dog Night . . .

And the closer, one Little Richard.

For a time, the promoters feared it would fall apart. Crosby, Stills and Nash and Johnny Winter pulled out and Joni Mitchell was showered with boos and stormed off after three songs. The emcee also quit, as did Canned Heat's front man during the band's set. Unlike Woodstock, the vibe was not love and peace but sneers and complaints. According to plan, Richard was to earn his top-shelf paycheck by closing the festival on Sunday night with a final exclamation point. And, once again, none of the contemporary acts objected to that. They all owed Little Richard, who pointed out that he could hear himself in their songs—Creedence's "Travelin' Band," for example, was, he said, "just 'Long Tall Sally.'" (Actually, according to John Fogerty, it was a paean to "Good Golly, Miss Molly.") Joplin, a tremendous blues singer, attested that she couldn't wait to see Richard do his thing when he would follow her for the climax— though it's arguable how straight she could see, since as Richard recalled, "She had been sucking on that Southern Comfort bottle." Yet, even hammered, her guttural "cosmic blues" won her three standing ovations. And attention from a new fan—Richard.

Janis was, he would say, "fantastic." When watching her, he "became numb." "The lady works, and she's got all this soul, and it proved to me that God didn't give all the soul to the Black man."

As she exited the stage, the rain was pouring down; it was 10 o'clock; the crowd had thinned out. Eager to clear out, too, the promoters told Richard that Janis's performance was a fitting climax and that he need not go on. He could keep his pay with no further labor. But all that meant to him was a challenge to his pride. When they asked if he was sure he could follow Joplin, he answered, "I don't know anyone I can't follow." He only had time to don his white "glass suit," as he called his white duds with a mirrored satin jacket and gold lamé cape. Then, in the pitch dark of evening, the lights came on, bathing him as if in divine illumination while the rain streamed down his face.

"I started gleaming," he remembered, "and I just took over the show. I lit it up."

"Lucille" got him started but as the rain intensified and the crowd continued leaving, Bumps Blackwell, who accompanied him to the event, recalled, "I thought for a minute that we'd bombed." Then, the vibe captured the people filing out, who began to groove on their parents' music. Within minutes, damp bodies were surging toward the stage, where security guards tried to wall them off. Richard allowed around a dozen to come up and dance on stage. Arousing the audience even more, Richard began shedding, as he said, "three thousand dollars' worth of clothes," including the cape, and throwing them into the mass of bodies. He was begged for two encores. The damp crowd didn't care what he sang. One of those there remembered that Richard "was electric," and at one point, "jumped off his piano, stripped off his spangly shirt, and went down on his knees to pray."

To Richard, it was more than just another day at the office. He would say, "it was like magic power came over—oh, Lord, of God, it was one of the greatest experiences," and that "It reminded me of 1956. I've never been on a show like this in all my life, in all the twenty years I've been in the business, I've never been on a show like this." Of the hippies, the mainly white suburban kids, many of whom had not heard of him, some not even born when he began, he blessed them as "the real people." If it wasn't 1956, at least he had, as *Rolling Stone* put it, "revived his own legend." Although no video was made of the festival, word of mouth was enough, creating more sellout gigs.

He didn't get an invite for Woodstock, but at another big venue days after Atlantic City—the Schaefer Music Festival in Central Park's Wollman Rink—*Rolling Stone* reported, "he came out in a red velvet suit with a gold embroidered jacket, prancing up and down like an exhibitionist talking to the kids, posing to let chicks take his picture, his 'wings held high,' throwing kisses, camping about, and right away starting to take off his clothes, 'You want my vest?'— takes it off and throws it into the audience. 'All you want is my vest?' he asks incredulously, pointing to his velvet pants. The audience shrieks, and Little Richard comes back: 'Shut up! I rather do it myself!'"

If much of America had lost track of him, the new rock press, founded by Baby Boomers bred in his era, had a soft spot for him, an old-timer who was also an oracle of rock's impending glam-and-glitter period. As he said, "The young people were raving over my outfits. I was way before my time. Back then they were calling me all kinds of sissies and freaks and faggots because I wore these things. Now all the groups are wearing them. Everybody's got a makeup kit in their band now." Such wit and wisdom would permeate his interviews, which were many. In 1970, he made the cover of *Rolling Stone*. The title of the interview within was succinct and perfectly accurate:

"Little Richard: Child of God."

*   *   *

IN HIS EARLY forties this child of heavenly heralds had lived not
even half his life, and he had more cat's lives to come. Already written was a remarkable story of constant redemption, with events far
and wide to come and go like highway signs seen through the wind-
shield of a car going a hundred miles an hour. Another era of soul
music took hold, that of kicky funk pop and string-laden romantic
R&B. Acid rock was reordered by hickory-flavored country rock
and soul—one avatar being the Allman Brothers Band, a herd of
blues-based white boys from Jacksonville, who would later make
their home in the epicenter of '50s and '60s soul, the Macon long
abandoned by Little Richard and James Brown.

In the midst of all this manic change, the originator himself was
very, very much alive. The year that the new decade dawned, he was
on both Dick Cavett's and David Frost's TV talk shows, and on
variety series by the Smothers Brothers, Andy Williams, and Bar-
bara McNair. He also signed on with his latest record company—
appropriately—Reprise, established by Frank Sinatra in 1960 as a
vehicle to sing his own recordings his way, bringing to the label his
Rat Pack and old big band cronies like Bing Crosby and Duke Ellington. Ol' Blue Eyes sold the label (which as part-owner he continued to record for) to Warner Brothers in '63 and its president Mo
Ostin signed rock acts like the Kinks and, by the new decade, Neil
Young, Joni Mitchell, T. Rex, and Jimi Hendrix. Ostin, another of
Richard's legion of fans, gave him sufficient money and the freedom
to produce his new material and he went into The Record Plant
studio in L.A. for the first of two sessions to record his first album
in three years. A follow-up session was scheduled when Richard was
on tour in the South, at Wishbone Studios in Muscle Shoals, one
of three legendary rock and soul factories in the Alabama woods.

For these sessions, Richard employed some of the finest musicians in the South, including guitarist Albert Lowe, sax man Ronnie Eader, and drummer Roger Hawkins. Some would call the work Richard's "country" album, and he did indulge a longtime fondness for the idiom, effortlessly covering Hank Williams's "Lovesick Blues." But it was more a thick coating of Southern blues, soul and funk, made familiar by Richard's now-strained screams. He cut two new songs he wrote. The title track—"The Rill Thing"—was a sinewy slow-jam instrumental as good a free-form blues rock/soul piece as any by Johnny Winter. The second was the disco-suited "Somebody Saw You." He also employed Memphis and Muscle Shoals guitarists Travis Wammack and Larry Lee, the latter of whom had backed Hendrix on guitar at Woodstock. Wammack's "Greenwood, Mississippi" was a Creedence-flavored tune with a blistering guitar solo that had Richard sounding like a male Tina Turner, while Lee's "Two-Time Loser" used riffs from Otis Redding's "I Can't Turn You Loose."

Richard also wrote, with Blackwell and Maybelle Jackson, the funky "Spreadin' Natta, What's the Matter?" And he summoned his old influence Esquerita to cowrite "Dew Drop Inn," saluting the club where Richard had wowed Blackwell with "Tutti Frutti," and Richard's "message song"—"Freedom Blues," which borrowed much from the Rascals' "People Got to Be Free," casting himself as an "old man" who had fulfilled "my duty, rock and roll." Another echo of Redding, the intro and hook "na-na-na-na-na-na-na-na" was a cop of Otis's famous "fa-fa-fa-fa-fa-fa" refrain. The message: he was ready to end "these freedom blues . . . everybody, everyone's gonna be free." For good measure there was even a prescient jab at the odious Richard Nixon, still in his first term and untainted by scandal—"Let's get rid of that old man, hey-ey-ey / And bring our government up to date." The final track was his Southern soul treatment of the Beatles' "I Saw Her Standing There."

It was a gas, arguably his finest work since his salad days, something like a concept album under the context of "Freedom Blues," which was released as a single in April and made a nifty run to number forty-seven on the pop chart and twenty-eight on the R&B. The album, its jacket decked out with an array of Little Richard photos in various poses both wild and introspective, came out in August along with "Greenwood, Mississippi" and won rave reviews, *Rolling Stone* gushing that "As incredible as it may seem, Little Richard is as great as he says he is." Yet the abiding contradiction of Little Richard held. "Freedom Blues" was clearly a step forward for him, and received play—but only on the white, album-oriented FM stations, while the urban black stations passed on it, only elevating the anger he had that his natural audience turned its back on him (after having complained that he was being sold only to the black audience). As a result, a very fine album was left on the shelf, and "Greenwood" had to fight to get to number eighty-five on the pop chart—not making the R&B chart at all, which seemed almost punitive given how little sense it made. Still, Richard, who had been missing from the black celebrity chorus of the Civil Rights movement, made no bones that the song's point wasn't narrowly focused.

"It's a message I want the whole world to hear," he explained. "I want the black power, the red power, the white power, the brown power, the green power to listen because this is what we need—get rid of those freedom blues."

REPRISE WAS HAPPY enough with the reviews and the profit margin for *Rill Thing,* and Richard was back in the Hollywood studio in May 1971, cutting his next album, modestly titled *The King of Rock and Roll.* The problem was, title notwithstanding, this serving was not fit for a king. None of the songs were written by him, most covers of rock and soul standards—"Dancing in the Street," "Brown Sugar," "Born on the Bayou," "Joy to the World," "The Way You Do the Things You Do," with one more teary Hank Williams cover, "I'm So Lonesome I Could Cry." The title track, one of two songs written by H.B. Barnum, was "Good Golly, Miss Molly" retrofitted, with Richard impishly insisting that he, "the man from Macon," was the king returned from exile, name-checking Elvis, Creedence, Sly Stone, Aretha, Ike and Tina, and Tom Jones as loyal subjects. It was fetching, but the bizarre decision to drop Richard's piano licks from the orchestrations took out much of his persona and the album stiffed.

By felicity, though, Hollywood once again came to his aid. The movies had turned to rock as a lure for the disposable dollars of affluent Baby Boomers, as well as black viewers drawn to the first wave of "gangsta" funk that came with "blaxploitation" movies like *Shaft* and *Super Fly*. That Little Richard was aligned with the former audience, and persona non grata with the latter, was one of the strangest contradictions in modern music. But it kept him marketable. In 1972, when Quincy Jones became musical director for the big-budget Warren Beatty–Goldie Hawn comedy *$*, he enlisted Richard to sing the title song, "Money Is," which was cut in the unabashedly wild style of his oldies.

As he aged further, his pretty face and lithe anatomy not showing a bit of erosion, he rarely stopped moving, the days, weeks, years, decades, and eras a blur, a confluence of the best and worst moments in history, many more of which were to come. By '72, Morrison, Hendrix, and Joplin were killed by self-inflicted excess, and two years after that, a president would resign for his own just as the cursed war in Vietnam would wind down and end in a whimper, in humiliating defeat for withering American hubris.

But Little Richard's oldies were always ready to let the good times roll. Although George Lucas's epic valentine to the '50s *American Graffiti* had no Little Richard songs—a high crime owing to Lucas and Specialty Records being unable to agree on a licensing fee—Richard was a mandatory player when Columbia Pictures released a 1973 film of an elaborate "Rock and Roll Revival" oldies tour that also featured Chuck Berry, Bo Diddley, Fats Domino, Bill Haley, and Chubby Checker. It earned more than $1 million and spawned a double-LP soundtrack album, but it also was a prism of the exodus of African Americans from rock and roll's original formulation—a disconnect that prompted *New York Times* film critic Vincent Canby to note the paucity of black fans on the tour and conclude that "there are no black memories of the 1950s." That, too, was a tragedy, and Little Richard had to make his peace with it. At the same time, he was in demand with the white rock crowd, and was called in to spice up records by acts such as Delaney & Bonnie, Mylon LeFevre (on his cover of the antiwar "He's Not Just a Soldier"), Joe Walsh's James Gang, Hot Tuna, and Canned Heat.

Mo Ostin was still down with footing Richard's sessions well into 1972, linking him up with some of L.A.'s top side men, including pedal steel guitarist Sneaky Pete Kleinow, baritone sax man Jim Horn, and guitarist Mike Deasy. Richard would invite Bumps Blackwell to coproduce his next Reprise album and re-employed old J&M studio confreres Lee Allen and Earl Palmer. He wrote four new songs and cowrote four others. In step with the times, five tracks for the album ran over five minutes, two of them, "Nuki Suki" and "Sanctified, Satisfied Toe-Tapper," instrumentals (with Richard muttering "Gimme some, gimme some, gimme some" on the former) extending for over five and seven minutes, respectively. In tone, the songs reeked of cliched '70s dance music, with prickly, syncopated drumming, funked-up guitars, and wailing saxes.

"Mockingbird Sally," the first cut, was a "Lucille"-type throwback rock jam; "Second Line" a near-spoken Richard dance rap; "The Saints" a cop of "The Saints Go Marching In" (with Richard stealing the writer's credit); "Prophet of Peace" a hip rap/rock sermon with a rambling, rap against war and racism, and to always keep on keepin' on—"You may not be an angel but you can fly." But Richard was so focused on getting everything right that the overall vibe lacked, well, soul. The album, *The Second Coming*, came with a striking Ed Thrasher cover photograph of Little Richard's sweaty face, half-hidden by drooping hair, his toothy smile blinding. Rolled out in September 1972, Richard went on the *Merv Griffin Show* to promote it. But then the critics had at the album, calling it well-meaning but overproduced, *Rolling Stone* giving it an "unfavorable." Weeks later it was gone, not charting. In November, "Mockingbird Sally" appeared as the first new Richard single in over a year, and it disappeared without a trace.

Suddenly, Ostin was less enchanted with updating Little Richard. He had bigger fish in his frying pan. Under the Warner/Reprise banner, he had moved up the ladder, gaining ascent with white rockers like Jackson Browne, Linda Ronstadt, Neil Young, and the Eagles. (He would chair the Warner/Elektra/Asylum conglomerate for thirty-two years and was elected to the Rock and Roll Hall of Fame in 2003.) With the pressure for success constant, his radar screen had little room for Richard as a wishful Lazarus. This became evident when he pulled the plug on what was to be one more Little Richard album, culled from a backlog of tapes. This one was slated to be Richard's full-blown "country" album; he would be positioned, as the title had it, as a *Southern Child*, wallowing in mud and moonshine but with panache. Pictures for the jacket had him in full Richard rhinestone regalia milking a cow in his backyard. All ten tracks were written either by Richard alone or in collaboration, one of the latter, a scratchy-voiced road song, "California (I'm Comin')" written with Ostin's son Randy, who worked promotions for Warner.

The title track was a jug-band-style rag that had him mock-drawling, "I'm a Southern child from down in Macon, Georgia" who was "trying to bring my baby back home." Singing in higher than usual keys, he managed to approximate the adenoidal range of the country rockers while keeping rooted to the grit of soul on cuts like "Burning Up With Love," "If You Pick Her Too Hard (She Comes Out of Tune)," "I Git a Little Lonely," and "Puppy Dog Song," a slow funk rap which ran to almost nine minutes with barking dogs providing the backup vocals (its first half was as close to modern rap as any song from that era). Whether it was goodly or goofy was debatable, but moot since no one would hear any of the tracks, not until they would be included in the 2004 three-CD Rhino box set *Little Richard—King of Rock and Roll: The Complete Reprise Recordings*.

That injunction pushed him out the Reprise door. As Richard told it in his authorized biography, "I left Reprise because [they] didn't have me at heart" and "didn't push" the records. "It was almost like someone had said, 'Hold Richard back.' So I left them. It wasn't mutual." Cutting slack to Ostin, he instead blamed "the producer" of the album, though that happened to be himself. He also fell back on a much-aired gripe, that radio stations were loath to play songs produced by black artists. As dubious this reasoning was, ignoring that the market for his new music simply wasn't there, it was one of the numerous reasons why he insisted, "Racism has always been so heavy against me in America."

* * *

RICHARD WAS IN no rush to record for yet another label. As it was, there was the ever-continuing repackaging of his golden oldies, not at the mercy of current music trends or critics. Despite his grudges against industry hands not sharing his vision, he had little thirst to try yet again at selling records to a market he didn't really understand. But his cachet was such that he could return to the studio merely as a lever for other aims. He recalled that when he was about to start a tour and "needed some money" for it, "Bumps and me got a deal for one album with an advance of ten thousand dollars . . . . We went in the studio and did it in one night."

These diversions might be studio cuts or live rerecordings of his oldies, and were issued by low-budget labels like Bell, United Artists (one of his records for them being a notable swamp-rock cover of Otis Redding's "Dock of the Bay," recorded at Muscle Shoals), Joy, Main, the TV mail-order label K-Tel, World, Kent, Green Mountain, Manticore, Mainstream, and Creole. None of these odds and ends amounted to much. And yet he still had a leg up on the other '50s soul men who could not hope to compete with an ever-changing rock, and unlike Richard did not even try. (Though Chuck Berry did find a way to update in 1972 with a live cover of Dave Bartholomew's 20-year-old novelty "My Ding-a-Ling," a sophomoric anthem to masturbation that, astonishingly, was his only number one pop song.)

If there were any song that Little Richard by rights should have recorded, it was *that* song. But he shunned superficiality in favor of heavy goals shaped by his whims. And even on the nostalgia circuit, he was just as adamant about top billing and the closing spot. "I hadn't been in the business all these years to let Jerry Lee get top billing over me," he said. And when a Jerry Lee or a Chuck did land the closing, he said, "Bumps and me got together to decide what to do. We planned to kill him dead."

Naturally, he was relentlessly self-promoting, even if what he promoted came from his imagination, such as saying that he was about to appear on Ed Sullivan or host a CBS TV special and that the Beatles had "just made me a very big offer to come with [their designer label] Apple Records." Still, veracity hardly mattered in the swirl of Little Richard, given that he would regularly be on the tube, on Carson, on Mike Douglas, on Sonny and Cher, on the Grammy Awards, on *The Midnight Special.* And this was the basic blueprint of his existence through most of the '70s, which went by in a blur, lost in a drug-fueled haze, and had serious repercussions. At a huge 1972 oldies show in London's cavernous Wembley Stadium, part of a long European tour, he and Chuck Berry shared top billing, putting Richard in a foul mood, giving rise to stories in the papers that he was feuding with Chuck, who he branded "old black Berry." Though he did not set his piano on fire this time, during his set Richard pouted, sang off-key, and suddenly stopped and sat atop his piano in stony silence, setting off a storm of booing and leaving promoters furious.

That tour would end in figurative flames. Believing the promoters were underpaying him, he crept into one of their offices and hid under the desk until the guy came in and he leaped out demanding money. He also claimed that because the promoters were inflating his earnings to the British Inland Revenue agency, he was dunned for $8,000 in back taxes. The promoters even refused to pay his way back home with his band. From then on, he would demand full pay from promoters, up front. In England, though, the gravy train was over. Promoters would not book him there. And, back home, his bookings dried up mainly because he wanted to do little more than inhale, pop, inject, or snort what Larry Williams was supplying him

SNATCHED FROM THE BURNING

with; when he did go on TV, he was high as a kite, even if it was hard to tell any difference from his usual frothing at the mouth. To his credit, he knew he didn't want Leva Mae and his siblings to see him like this, and so he began spending his time in L.A. living out of a cheap Sunset Boulevard bungalow where Caligula reemerged, with Richard carving out new heights of carnality.

For these boogie days and nights, Lee Angel reentered his life, although he would normally have three of four girls in his room so he could watch them, as he put it, "do anything." He also spoke of having painful anal sex with "a boy." At that point, he said, homosexuality had "take[n] over [my] whole life" and that it "demoralize[d] me." The drugs were the backdrop. By his reckoning, he had "deteriorated. . . . I weighed about a hundred fifteen pounds. All I was interested in doing was getting high. I'd be riding all over L.A. looking for cocaine. They shoulda called me Little Cocaine, I was sniffing so much of the stuff! Every time I blew my nose there was flesh and blood on my handkerchief, where it had eaten out my membranes."

Add to that weed, angel dust, and the heroin he mixed with coke—"speed-balling," the practice that killed John Belushi. Eventually blowing around a thousand dollars a day, he couldn't pay Larry Williams for fronting him his stash, and Williams—who had degenerated into a crazed thug—came looking for his old idol, with a gun.

"Richard," he told him, "I'm gonna kill you. Ain't no one going to mess around with my money."

Calling that "the most fearful moment in my life," Richard said he was able to scrounge up the money, but the incident jarred him into facing the reality of a life now in tatters, shattered.

*   *   *

THE FACE HE saw staring vacantly back at him in the mirror should have scared him straight. He had become nasty, combative, self-pitying, the cocaine having made him paranoid that someone was lurking around the next corner waiting to harm him. He hired a phalanx of bodyguards. When he was on the road, they became his drug mules.

On those travels, his retinue grew to a dozen people, swelled by managers, valets, a bookkeeper, and various leeches and yes-men. But he would be by himself in his hotel room, snorting or shooting. Richard would say the drugs made him realize "what homosexuality had made me." That was the great bugaboo of his life, and now, in his guilt, he said, "I wanted to hurt. I wanted to kill." His troupe was so terrified that they wouldn't come into the room, even to get paid.

In his agitated state of mind, he again turned on Bumps Blackwell, blaming him for his money woes and not the drugs. Saying he couldn't trust him, he canned Blackwell for the third, and last, time. The timing, according to Blackwell, was very bad on Richard's part, as Bumps would claim he had just negotiated an oldies circuit deal with promoter Richard Nader that would have paid Richard $10,000 per show, $125,000 in all. With Bumps out, the deal collapsed. In any case, the split marked the end of the dynamic duo that had made peerless rock and roll history, and for Blackwell the core of his obituary when he died in 1985 at age 66.

Richard formed a management company with his brothers Marquette, Robert, and Peyton. They called it Bud Hole, which was not a winking allusion to "butt hole" but rather their father's nickname (the hole part was not clear). The troika found him some residual gigs but he seemed burned out. After a grueling week-long Radio

City Music Hall run in October 1975, he began '76 with shows at the American Hotel in Miami, the Hyatt in L.A., and the Richfield Coliseum in Ohio. Then, running on empty, he returned to the hotel, still not ready to change ways. Rather, thinking he could ease the mental and physical pain by numbing himself with whatever chemical on hand, he went into a frightful shell of isolation back home. Even Lee Angel couldn't break through it.

"I was so shocked," she said. "In the early days I had barely seen him take a drink." Now, "He'd gotten into drinking, smoking and drugs in a big way. He just wasn't himself. He didn't know how to hold a cigarette, yet he was smoking." Once, when the ash fell off the cigarette Richard was smoking and landed on his lap, he remarked, "Ah! So that's how a Negro smells when he's burning. I wonder how a female might—"

Not letting him finish the sentence, Angel tore into him: "We got into this heavy fight. Because I could hear him thinking, what happens if I burn Angel?" At that point, he was so scarred, it seemed possible he could commit violence, possibly even kill himself. He was almost surely in a death spiral, headed for the same fate as Hendrix. Then, in late 1976, he was hit head-on by what he took as a sign from God as powerful as his "Sputnik" epiphany had been.

Actually, it was a series of signs, measures of how tenuous life is. First, one of his valets was murdered in the home of a heroin dealer. Then a friend named Curly Knight was killed by a street gang. Then, after a night of cocaine-overload partying, he awoke to learn his brother Tony had died of a heart attack while watering his lawn, leaving a wife and young son. That, he said, was "the saddest moment of my life." Stunned as he was, he was stung by reality again when the son of a friend of the family was fooling around with a gun when it went off and killed him. This procession of heartbreak was a clear message from above; to Richard, it meant he was next in line. He had lived with premonitions of an early death, and now it seemed the stage was set.

Tony's death hit him the hardest and, looking back, he said he took it as a door opening and that he could either walk through it or go up in flames. "I opened my Bible at 'Mark 36', where God says: 'What shall it profit a man if he should gain the whole world and lose his own soul?'" When he walked through, he said, God had "snatched me from the burning." The first thing he did was to tell his mother he was quitting show business again and would finally do what he set out to do in 1957. Moving back in with Leva Mae, he went cold turkey and lived in his old room reading his Bible, diligently enough to finally fulfill that long-eluded life goal of becoming a minster. Unlike the first withdrawal, there would be no notices of his activities, no teasing of any comeback. The last of his throwaway records, redoes of "Good Golly, Miss Molly"/"Rip It Up," released by Creole in 1977, went unnoticed and no sessions loomed on the horizon. Meanwhile, Little Richard was again washing feet. "When Tony died," said Lee Angel, "Richard just snapped. That was the end of all the drugs. He went into selling Bibles. I got a call not long after and I went up to see him in Los Angeles. It took me a moment to recognize him. The pompadour had gone. His hair was like it was when he was young. He was wearing a suit and tie. And I saw my Richard again."

Singing only for the benediction of the Lord, he doubled back to gospel and inspiration. After being ordained by the Seventh-day Adventist Church, his parish the Universal Remnant Church of God, he still had the itch to sing and called Joe Lutcher to get the old revival act together. But Lutcher was firmly out of the business and Richard went on the road with Elder Everett L. Rainey, a church pastor in Arkansas, playing tent shows and church masses. His income, however, was mainly from selling *The Black Heritage*

Bible, highlighting black biblical figures, for $24.95. If he was living humbly, he was more fortunate than Larry Williams. In 1980, at age 44, the man who was groomed to replace Little Richard as the biggest name in rock, was found in his home with a bullet in his head. His death was barely noticed, ruled a suicide despite having given many a reason to want him dead. Richard, forgiving him for threatening to kill him, attended the funeral, genuinely sad for his old friend, but no doubt aware that but for the grace of God the man being lowered into the cold earth could easily have been him.

THAT WAS MORE than forty years ago. In the eternity since, there would be wavering, clarifications, contradictions, rationalizations, revisions, relapses, and painful interludes, but not a full-scale reversion to the obsessions that created timeless art and personal anguish. Because people would ask about his gay past, Little Richard found himself renouncing homosexuality albeit with an uneasy hedge—his philosophy being racial and gender inclusion. This revelation came wrapped inside a larger one, a newfound respect for women. "I never knew I could like women," he said. "I never knew there'd be a day when I didn't want to have a man." He made these subjects part of his preaching. Yet he did not remarry, stopping his proposals to Lee Angel when she moved to England and married a wealthy man. He found the most contentment being alone. In the early '80s, he moved back to a hotel, the Hyatt in L.A., living pretty much incognito. He charted his daily routine as, "I wake up and worship. I get on my knees. I pray. I thank God for the activity of my limbs. Then I order room service."

Other than a slapdash gospel album of four tracks, including the old hymn "I Surrender All," recorded in Nashville—released by

World Records in 1979 as *God's Beautiful City* with side two a pair of his sermons—there was only radio silence from Little Richard. He did go into an L.A. studio in '81 for a session he paid for, but it was aborted after two gospel songs. The only sighting of him was when he appeared on *American Bandstand's* 30th anniversary special that same year, to congratulate Dick Clark. However, in his sermons, he had no praise for rock and roll, which he now called "demonic . . . taken from voodoo, from the voodoo drums." Absolving himself, he averred that "God permitted me to be famous for a reason," his voice able to turn the world "from Rock 'n' Roll to the Rock of Ages—to get ready for eternal life."

His family was relieved that he had finally found his way. And Richard made a promise to Leva Mae that he would never again backslide and sing rock and roll. He intended to keep that vow, which he considered sacred. In 1984 he agreed to an authorized biography written by English radio host Charles White, a Little Richard fanatic who pitched the project to him and landed a handsome advance. Richard saw it as a way to preach to a wide audience but although a good half of the book included excruciating full-scale sermons and attestations of faith, and renunciations of his sexual deviations, these pages likely went unread while readers pored over his meticulously detailed, run-on anecdotes of his "pumping" and peeping behavior. All of which reawakened the public's image of him as a prodigious, unapologetic, half-loony satyr—only inflating his brand even more. (He would wallow in it, pushing the book in numerous interviews as a great landmark in literature—but he sheepishly admitted that he had not seen White's manuscript, hinting that not all of it was necessarily true, which lent credence to Lee Angel's denials of how she was portrayed.)

While he testified in the book that "I can never see myself going back to rock 'n' roll," the immediate effect of its success was that his music was subject to another round of tribute—which was always like the high of a drug in itself—and that he would need to go back to the "demonic" format after all, in some manner he could rationalize. That still seemed a long way off when, just before the book was published, Leva Mae died, sending him into another tailspin. So grievous was her death that he couldn't bear to even set foot in the house, breaking down and sobbing just looking into her empty bedroom. But the obligation he had to sell the book dragged him to his feet, doing guest shots on the TV talk circuit, going on David Letterman, Phil Donahue, and on the BBC.

The publicity he garnered did no less than reawaken his dormant legend, and he became a pop culture fixture all over again. *Saturday Night Live*'s lone megastar in the early '80s, the young Eddie Murphy, mimicked Richard perfectly in skits, alloying him with the then-popular, and equally flouncing diet guru, in a character called "Little Richard Simmons." On the Letterman show, Richard couldn't resist singing "Tutti Frutti," a major step back into inevitable revival. Not even his vows to God and Leva Mae could dampen that movement, which became a full leap when Mo Ostin, sensing that the market for Little Richard had ripened, reentered and offered him a one-album deal, on the Warner label that Richard had complained he had been excluded from before. With Richard about to go on a book tour in England, a session was arranged for him in September 1984 in Surrey.

By then, things were popping all over for him. The director/producer Paul Mazursky offered him a small but memorable role in his newest movie *Down and Out in Beverly Hills*, as well as having him write and perform a song for the soundtrack. The result was "Great Gosh A'mighty (It's a Matter of Time)," a wall-banger he wrote with Billy Preston, deliriously bridging gospel and rock. He brought Preston to England along with several of the Nashville musicians he had recorded with to back him up on the Warner album, which would include "Gosh A'mighty," the tracks overseen by British producer Stuart Coleman. Thus, in the blink of an eye, he was back in the rock and roll center ring, which he justified by saying "I believe that some rock 'n' roll is real bad but I believe there is some not as bad," those exceptions being songs that were "positive, elevating, wholesome and uplifting" and that "makes you think clearly."

This left a lot of room for subjectivity, and if he felt at all guilty about going back on his word to Leva Mae he had little time to think about it. He was in such demand that as soon as the album, *Lifetime Friend*, was done he was on a plane back for the twelve-hour flight to L.A. for the funeral of one of his lifetime friends, Rock Hudson, who had just died from AIDS, the scourge that was scaring America to death—and which led Richard, who would lose too many other friends to the disease, to break from the ignorance of his church brethren and not blame gay men's behavior for them contracting it. He also was scheduled to film a bit part on the hit NBC show *Miami Vice* as a preacher in a dazzling white suit who gave fiery anti-drug sermons—a natural for him, to be sure, and proof that Little Richard 3.0 was still cool in his fifties.

However, bad luck always seemed around the corner. And it was, literally. After he filmed his part, exhausted from his long flights and work load, he got behind the wheel of his Cadillac, fell asleep while driving—which he rarely did, for reasons like this—and smashed into a telephone pole. Badly injured, he had to be cut from the wreckage and wheeled into an ambulance, a frightful scene shown on the news that night. He would spend three months in the hospital, with thirty-six steel pins implanted in his mangled right leg. During his confinement, no less than Bob Dylan sat at his bedside easing the ordeal. He came out with a limp and severe pain in the leg that would be permanent, but otherwise he was still on his track. Mazursky, pleased with "Great Gosh A'mighty," filmed his scene in *Down and Out in Beverly Hills* as Richard Dreyfuss's silk-robe-clad, record producer neighbor Orvis Goodnight, whose outraged rantings were a hoot—again no great stretch for Little Richard, who knew something about being down and out and hilariously ranting. His best line, delivered with relish, was: "I know why I don't get the protection I'm supposed to get—I'm black! Ain't no black man supposed to live in Beverly Hills!" It was a five-minute performance worthy of an Oscar.

Preceding the movie's release, the single reached number forty-two on the pop chart in April, the highest he'd been on it since 1958. *Lifetime Friend* didn't chart but put two songs on the British pop list. It wasn't the same as 1956, but for all intents and purposes, Little Richard was back, occupying a space compatible with the major zones of influence in entertainment. Indeed, one could argue that, with his reemergence in the public eye on movie screens, he was now more in the loop as the actor playing Little Richard than the singer singing Little Richard.

HIGH AND A-MIGHTY as he was, Richard had decided it was time to go after what he had been long deprived of, the royalties from his songs. His lawyers had begun legal proceedings against Art Rupe and Specialty Records, seeking to audit the books to determine just how much he was owed. When they got the numbers, they realized that the settlement Richard had signed in the late '50s was one of the worst rip-offs ever of a performer. "The very thought of it was sickening to me now," Richard said at the time. "[Rupe] has made millions and he should owe me millions."

He filed a federal lawsuit, claiming he was owed $115 million, while Rupe, who would remain atop the company until it was sold in 1991, counter-sued, claiming that Richard accusing him of fraud was defamation.

Rupe was still making a profit off Little Richard; in 1983 Specialty released the long-vaulted "Chicken Little Baby" and "All Around the World." But, further complicating matters, in 1979 Rupe had sold the publishing rights to Richard's classic songs to ATV, the giant song publishing company, when he pawned off his publishing company Venice Music to them; thus, Richard's suit added ATV as codefendants. However, a judge dismissed the action, affirming Rupe's case that the '59 deal was binding. That would not be the end of the fight, however. Richard appealed. And, by coincidence, ATV would figure in another Little Richard scenario. In '85, Michael Jackson purchased ATV for $47.5 million, in order to become owner of the Beatles' songs in ATV's catalog. Only then did Jackson find he was also owner of thousands of other songs, including Little Richard's.

Richard and Michael had known each other well; Jackson was one of his legatees. A few years before, Richard recalled, Michael had "offered me a job with his publishing company [called Mijac] as a writer. At the time, I didn't take it. I wish I had." Now, however, Jackson went one better. He and his attorney John Branca worked out a deal with Richard to return to him not the publishing rights to his songs—as has been inaccurately reported—but a generous sum, estimated at around $4 million, remunerating him for the years of income denied him. Jackson, who inexplicably got into money trouble as well, a year later sold half of ATV and Mijac to Sony, a partnership still in effect as of this writing, eleven years after Jackson's death. That conglomerate still owns the recurring profits from the Little Richard catalog. But Richard was no longer shut out; and in 1986, Rupe, perhaps feeling a pang of guilt in light of Jackson's largesse, came to a settlement with Richard for something like $1 million.

While the court battles had raged (as a sidebar, Rupe sued Creedence Clearwater Revival for plagiarizing Richard, and the band settled out of court), Richard turned to selective recording as part of his new iteration in the movie culture. Warner, though, did not benefit from "Great Gosh," which by dint of being on the *Down and Out* soundtrack album was licensed to MCA as a single. Hoping for a spillover effect, Warner failed to chart with two Richard singles, "Operator" and "Somebody's Coming," the latter in January 1987, convincing Ostin his investment in Little Richard was over. Not that Richard stewed about it. Instead, only a year later, he was back putting a fingerprint on another blockbuster, the title track of the absurd Arnold Schwarzenegger-Danny DeVito comedy *Twins*, in a duet with Earth, Wind and Fire's Philip Bailey. Produced by Rhett Lawrence, it marked Richard's entree into generic, soulless, '80s-style techno-pop. Released as a single from the soundtrack album licensed to CBS Records, it didn't chart but won a Golden Globe for best original song. The movie reeled in more than $200 million—meaning that Little Richard was on two soundtracks for movies that made more than $260 million; and one of the many films that used his oldies on their soundtracks, *The Mask*, made another $40 million.

There was no doubt he belonged now, yet the song "Twins" was the last single ever put out under the Little Richard brand. He was now an elder statesman not just of rock but the rock culture itself, not as a porcelain, aging icon like Chuck Berry and Jerry Lee Lewis but, without seeming to age at all, as a performer who could still hit a high squeal and prance atop his piano; his self-spoofed mincing and dialect still hitting the ground running. To be a legend and a hoot was a lifebuoy keeping him afloat, particularly in the movie niche, also recording with the Beach Boys a dreamy gospel-style ballad, "Happy Endings," which went to number forty-five on the pop chart and was used in the movie bomb *The Telephone*, and "Rock Island Line" backed by Fishbone on a Woody Guthrie and Lead Belly tribute LP.

When the industry's annual ritual of self-congratulation began in 1986, with the corporate nabobs of the not-yet-built Rock and Roll Hall of Fame inducting its first class, headed by Berry, Lewis, Elvis, James Brown, Ray Charles, Sam Cooke, Fats Domino, the Everly Brothers, Buddy Holly, and Little Richard, his induction speech was given by Roberta Flack. Richard was still recovering from his automobile crackup and couldn't travel to New York for the rites at the Waldorf Astoria Hotel, and instead sent a rollicking videotaped speech; he did the same when soon after he was inducted into the Songwriters Hall of Fame. But the following year, he was whole again and delivered the induction speech for Otis Redding, mixing in renditions of "I Can't Turn You Loose," "Dock of the Bay," "Fa-Fa-Fa-Fa-Fa (Sad Song)," and riffing, "Y'all gonna make me scream like a white lady!" and the obligatory "Shut up!" That night also saw the induction of the Beatles, when George Harrison gave props to the "rock and rollers, and Little Richard," saying with affection, "It was his fault, really." No one agreed more than Richard.

He also sang the oldies at a concert in Cleveland when the Hall opened its doors. In all these gigs, as well as those on TV singing or sitting on a couch when he reeled off his well-practiced lines such as "I'm still here and I look decent," he looked like a million bucks. And it mattered not a whit that record companies had no room for him. He had been there, done that. And so the time was right for another reformation, promising himself to the word of the Lord. The difference was, this time he would not even try to rationalize his acceptance of only certain kinds of rock and roll. To be sure, the old huffing about the devil's music was gone. Rock was no longer a renegade art, and was sung in church; and homosexuality was a third-rail issue only among the most rigid religious con men. Not even the AIDS epidemic and its resulting homophobic imprecations about being gay made a dent. Though he made a point to renounce homosexuality, he needn't have. In the '90s, Little Richard seemed harmless, even *mild*, though with a fixed role—as one rock scribe put it, to "define the classic rock and roll position . . . living outside society's mainstream, on the edge."

It was a malleable bubble Reverend Richard Penniman could live inside, and he could get quite prickly when skeptics had at him about his sincerity. After *Jet* ran a piece hinting that Richard was not totally serious about singing for the Lord again, he was livid. When the movie director John Waters then interviewed him for *Playboy* in 1987, Richard sensed Waters was similarly skeptical due to prattle about his sexual urges. He stopped the interview and demanded to pay Waters to turn over the tapes, threatening to sic his bodyguard on the writer if he didn't. Waters refused and the interview ran under the title "Little Richard, Happy at Last?" Richard was elated he had been anointed in *Playboy.* Such was the never-ending contradiction of Little Richard.

HE DID GET back to recording, in 1990 singing a duet with Jon Bon Jovi for the *Young Guns* movie soundtrack and the following year on a collective cause album, *Voices That Care,* supporting the troops in the brief Iraq War. In 1992, in another niche project for a huge conglomerate, Disney, he cut a novelty soft-rock version of the children's favorite "The Itsy Bitsy Spider." Disney broached him to cut an album of kiddie songs, called *Shake It All About*, including a redo of "Keep A-Knockin'" in the juvenile niche. His final studio album also came that year as a vanity project for the small Eastworld label, rerecording more of his classic hits in stripped-down format, accompanied by Japanese guitarist Masayoshi Takanaka. There were also duet tracks with Elton John, Tanya Tucker, Eddie Floyd, Jerry Lee Lewis on his *Last Man Standing* album (covering "I Saw Her Standing There"), Joe Walsh, famed gospel singer Dottie Rambo, and on a posthumous Johnny Cash tribute album.

As his songs played on, and on, he would pop in and out of sight, here and there, lighting up a stage, a movie, a TV special, a commercial with Michael Jordan, always playing himself either literally or by proxy. In 1993, still remarkably active, he received a Grammy for Lifetime Achievement, another make-good for having denied him and other pioneering black rockers their props—and their balance due—in real time.

Still, unable to keep from squandering money, even the surprising windfall from Michael Jackson couldn't keep him secure in his lifestyle. Director Ava DuVernay recalled when she was a waitress at a diner in L.A. at the time, Richard "tipped me a crisp $100 bill each week on a $75 breakfast with friends." He was not above indulging shlock for a paycheck, going so low as to open a Wrestlemania event at Madison Square Garden, wearing a red, white, and blue jumpsuit similar to James Brown's nouveau look while warbling "America the Beautiful." But nothing could undercut his appeal. He was a ubiquitous commodity, still a turn-key operation, his high-powered agent Dick Alen, who also represented Aretha Franklin, able to close a quick deal for him. In '99, he obtained for Richard a large cut for permission to film a two-hour NBC biopic of his life directed by Robert Townsend and starring the actor Leon, the vocals dubbed by the Temptations' Ali-Ollie Woodson; the drama, full of colloquial black idioms and circumspect about his sexuality, corralled positive reviews.

The 21st century saw Little Richard turn seventy, and as if to prove no moss was growing under his feet, he was spry and back on the road, touring America and Europe, selling out halls, still cheating the clock. He did one gig in Nashville, wearing rhinestone-spangled cowboy boots when given the Rhapsody & Rhythm Award by the National Museum of African American Music. By now, making up for lost time, he hired his sometimes rapper son, Danny Jones Penniman, as a bodyguard on his excursions. He was always up for a prominent event.

One final artifact was left for the new millennium: the 2005 drop of *Southern Child*, the long-shelved 1972 "country album" for Reprise, licensed to Rhino Records as a stereo LP and CD set, complete with the cover image of Richard milking a cow. But the Little Richard catalog, still making money for other people, was never at rest for long; compilation and repackaged albums popped up on Rhino and the niche Dimi Music Group label, in addition to the anthologies of Specialty, Vee-Jay, and Reprise—right up to 2016, when first a combo Specialty-Vee-Jay anthology, *Directly from My Heart*, then *Playlist: The Best of the Reprise Years,* came out on the Concord label.

He was still looking and sounding tight when he sang a duet with John Fogerty at the 2008 Grammy Awards, and when inducted a year later into the Louisiana Music Hall of Fame, sang with Fats Domino. But now time was not on his side. Hip replacement surgery laid him low, though he could raise the devil for a show here and there—such as at the Howard Theater in 2012 when, according to *Rolling Stone*, he was "full of fire, still a master showman, his voice loaded with deep gospel and raunchy power." He also did a stretch in Vegas.

Then, in 2013, when he confided to friends that he'd suffered a mild heart attack, he told *Rolling Stone*, "I am done" as a music man. He said that "Jesus had brought me through" and that whatever time he had left should be lived far from L.A., in seclusion. At first he took up residence in the Hilton Hotel in Nashville, where he performed his last engagement on August 20, 2014 (five days later he conducted a sermon/concert at South Church in Murfreesboro), then found solitude in Tullahoma, down the road twelve miles from Lynchburg, where Jack Daniel's is distilled. He soon needed help to get around and made peace with being wheelchair bound. To aid him, Danny moved in, and would wheel him onto a stage when Richard made an appearance.

His numerous albums, compilations, and box sets continued to sell. When a remastered version of his debut album *Here's Little Richard* was released in 2012, it won raves from rock critics, some not born until Richard was of Social Security age. Nearing his ninth decade, he finally seemed at ease with himself and his conscience, or at least with telling the latter to butt out. He had outlived all but one of his brothers and several of his doppelgangers, Michael Jackson, Prince, and Rick James. Among his rock and roll contemporary giants, he had outlived all but Chuck Berry and Jerry Lee Lewis, in what seemed like a private contest between the rock leviathans to see which would actually be standing last.

In 2017, when Chuck died at ninety and "The Killer" at eighty-two had used up far more chips from fate in health scares, financial crises, and personal tragedies than had even Richard, speculation began to mount that Little Richard had a foot in the grave. The great funk bassist Bootsy Collins visited him in 2017 and told a newspaper Richard "is not in the best of health," implying that the end was near. Bristling, Richard publicly insisted otherwise.

"Not only is my family not gathering around me because I'm ill," he said, knocking down one rumor, "but I'm still singing."

His lawyer William Sobel pronounced him "vivacious" and "still very active in a daily routine." He seemed to prove this when, his head beautifully bald and shining above his wraparound glasses, he went on a religious TV show and preached from his wheelchair for an hour, barely taking a breath. In small gatherings, he would still sing Sister Rosetta Tharpe songs and weave hilarious monologues about Macon and the characters who inspired so many songs. But he was keeping a secret. He had been diagnosed with bone cancer, hoping he could somehow beat it with prayer and luck, his biggest allies. Each day he made it through was a precious victory. And there were three more years of them.

Then, during the crisis when coronavirus swept through America, he confessed to Dick Alen that he was "not doing well," about as alarming a warning as the eternal optimist in him could issue. To be around family, he had his brother Robert move in with him.

And on the morning of May 9, 2020, Danny found him lifeless in his bedroom, having taken his last breath during his sleep.

As the killer virus was claiming lives around the world literally by the minute, one famous man's death by natural causes became the headline of the day. The outpouring of sympathy bore witness to the fact that a large piece of America's storied obsession with rock and roll had died with him. That day, internet searches for Little Richard rose dramatically and vintage videos of him on YouTube spiked. Radio stations received requests to play "Tutti Frutti" and the other evergreens.

The world grieved, and would again when he was laid to rest days later. A private funeral was held on the campus of Oakwood University in Huntsville, the pastoral school that had condemned his earthly excesses over sixty years ago now becoming the place where he was buried. In Macon, where a downtown street had been named for Little Richard in 1990, the city had moved the old Penniman house to a new location and renovated it as a landmark and museum in 2017. Upon his passing, calls increased for a downtown Confederate statue to be replaced by one of Little Richard. On an individual level, the most common reaction to his passing was to give yet one more listen to those old songs, imploring the soul to get busy ripping it up, shaking it up, and—even if still wishfully—balling tonight. It was the command Little Richard gave us all, en masse. Few have ever failed to hear it. If you can't hear it, can't feel it, all the way inside you, you can't feel anything. And if that's the case, then just—

Shut up!

EPILOGUE

"I HAD MY OWN THANG"

The testaments of sincere tribute began pouring in from around the globe the morning of May 9, 2020, from the rock and roll cognoscenti. Ringo Starr tweeted an old photo of the Beatles posed around Richard back in the Hamburg days when the Fab Four had to beg him to let them open for him. Brian Wilson noted that "Little Richard's music will last forever." Keith Richards averred that Richard "was the true spirit of Rock 'n' Roll!" Michelle Obama's tribute was perhaps the most trenchant: "We are so lucky to have had him."

It was certainly not unexpected. He had, after all, cheated the calendar nearly his entirely life, proudly and accurately boasting how "pretty" he was, reminding generation after generation bred on rock and roll that he had gotten there (almost) first as the pied piper of modern pop music and its culture. Although this book was written while he was alive, the possibility of his death always loomed over it. However, something about his constant rebirths and redemption made Little Richard seem as if he might live forever. Which is why the news of his passing, while logically not a surprise, was like losing a friend one never met but who seemed to have sung directly to you, rousing you to get up and get down and throw off the shackles of conventionalism. Even the bulletins of his passing had that effect. His music, always an elixir, now was more like holy water.

IN RETROSPECT, EVERYTHING about him was wild but also strategic. A gospel singer by choice, he had smartly understood what young audiences craved. Seeing him in old film clips, in images that stuck to him like glue, he is wild and crazy but in total control. Always, he knew his audience and what he could get away with. In the staid '50s, his *wooooo!* was the portal to something dark, dangerous, and irresistible. It was the mating call of rock and roll, proudly black and boldly lecherous music rushing into the mainstream when life for black men like Richard included being fitted for a rope around the neck. Even so, his weapon of choice wasn't a sledgehammer but a playful wink. In truth, no one was *less* threatening than Little Richard as he worked the Liberace playbook of kitschy gender ambiguity in an America stuck in Cold War, middle-class conventionality, when children were rebelling and existing moral codes were being put on notice. And as it played out, his music would be the soundtrack of end times. As such, it will still be played when this strained, clay and granite planet falls apart.

In all great modern pop music, colloquialisms become dated, but life's great driving forces don't: sex, love, conquest, laughter, profit, and sex. With a new Little Richard vinyl gem coming out seemingly every week, there were thirty-seven Little Richard singles in the decade of the 1950s that altered America. The sad postscript being that as rock has gotten more serious and less titillating, it has lost what was its very climbing tree—its soul.

BLACK PERFORMERS LIVED on a different kind of plantation in the 1950s. Bound within the straitjacket of "race music," being denied full mainstream acceptance, meant record sales would be limited, revival dependent on white disc jockeys hearing the call of the future. While Little Richard racked up fourteen Top 10 hits on the *Billboard* R&B chart, including three number ones—"Long Tall Sally," "Rip It Up," and "Lucille"—he notched only two Top 10 hits on the *Billboard* Top 100. When the Grammy Awards were first awarded in 1959, even enormous sales could not lead to black rockers being nominated for Song of the Year or Record of the Year. By the '70s, the partitions had been torn down and one of Richard's numerous legatees, Stevie Wonder, was winning multiple Grammys seemingly every year, at one time concurrently holding the number-one spot on *four* separate *Billboard* charts. By then, Little Richard's hit-making days were long over but his influence was cemented forever.

Even decades after his soul brothers had left the stage, ceding it to the rappers, he proclaimed, "I invented hip-hop!" No matter that he himself didn't ever sing it, woe be anyone who cares to argue the point. Or with John Waters's epitaph upon the news of Little Richard's death, that "He was the first punk. He was the first everything . . . a great figure of rebellion and sexual confusion" (who had also, Waters noted, died "completely homophobic and saying terrible things about gay people and transgender people").

In countless ways, Little Richard was more of a lightning rod than even he knew. But all that ever really mattered to him was that people were listening. From the start, he knew why they would.

"I always did have that thang," he said. "I didn't know what to do with that thang. I had my own thang I wanted the world to hear. If you hear a funny tone in my voice, that's the Angeltown sound."

MODERN ROCK CONSTANTLY recycled him, reaffirming his place in its inner sanctum. Typical was a 2010 *Rolling Stone* list of the "Greatest Singers" in rock history placing him twelfth—one slot ahead of Roy Orbison, one behind Paul McCartney, two behind James Brown, the magazine attesting that Richard's "falsetto shrieks demolish[ed] the rules of pop singing," and citing John Lennon's quote that when he first heard "Long Tall Sally," he "didn't want to leave Elvis, but this was so much better."

Beyond the belated laurels of rock's white corporate power structures, the great soul men of rock were interlocked, all able to proudly command—as Otis Redding demanded—r-e-s-p-e-c-t. Each was, as Chuck Berry cast himself, a "brown-eyed handsome man," possessed of a unique musical vision. Little Richard's distinction was that he broke big first, establishing a template that Chuck modified, moving to the forefront his wicked, clanging guitar interwoven with Richard-style piano triplets of the incomparable Johnnie Johnson. Chuck would say he wanted to do with his guitar what Richard did with his voice—the identical explanation given a decade later by Jimi Hendrix about his guitar. And Little Richard would say that Chuck's "rhythm is the only one I can sing my songs to" besides his own. (Though he covered Jerry Lee Lewis and Fats Domino songs, he never did a Chuck Berry record, nor did Berry any of his.)

To be certain, sounding like Little Richard—or trying to— welded dozens of singers. That included Jerry Lee and Elvis, who chose "Ready Teddy" to sing on his third appearance on *The Ed Sullivan Show* in 1956, drawing around 50 million pairs of eyeballs, giving Richard's song an audience it never could have received otherwise. Buddy Holly covered the tune, too, and there have been updated versions reaching into even the heavy-metal crowd, rewritten by the Rods as "Rock Hard" and Whitesnake as "Ready to Rock," the latter fitted with lines such as "I'm running so hot / I'm getting ready to shoot my shot."

Not for nothing can his influence be heard in the music of James Brown, Otis Redding, Mick Jagger, Wilson Pickett, Solomon Burke, David Ruffin . . . anyone, really, who was moved to sing by Little Richard. Both John Lennon and McCartney have said he was the muse that ignited their musical ambitions, Paul recalling that "Long Tall Sally" was the first rock and roll song he ever sang in public. Richard's influence could be literally transmuted to succeeding generations, in covers of his hits, in bits and pieces tucked into other songs (e.g., Mitch Ryder's "Devil With a Blue Dress/Good Golly Miss Molly"), and in name-checks such as Robert Parker's lyrical inclusion of "Long Tall Sally" in "Barefootin'"). If Paul McCartney's primal screams in "I Saw Her Standing There," "I'm Down," "She's a Woman," "Lady Madonna," and "Oh! Darling" have a familiar ring, it is not by chance; he's channeling Little Richard, who could never have sung a polemic like "Revolution" but wound up in it anyway, in McCartney's long intro screech.

Nor would he have delivered a James Brown–like political punch by singing anything like "Say It Loud, I'm Black and I'm Proud." He simply lived it. His joyous exhortations of (and later recording of the song titled) "Great gosh a'mighty!," plucked from the Negro spiritual "Free At Last," were roughly Martin Luther King's final words of the "I Have a Dream" speech: "Great God almighty, we're free at last."

If he didn't pander to "black power," he lived it, flaunted it, having thrived despite ingrained racism, both in his prime and thereafter, when in an unlikely turn the black audience abandoned him. Not that it deterred him. How could it?

"I believe my music can make the blind see, the lame walk, the deaf and dumb hear and talk," he once said, believing every word, "because it inspires and uplifts people. I've had old women tell me I made them feel they were nineteen years old. It uplifts the soul, you see everybody's movin', they're happy, it regenerates the heart and makes the liver quiver, the bladder splatter, the knees freeze."

Amen, Brother Richard. And we know the next line, because it was always the last line:

Hallelujah, childr'n! Hallelujah!

BIBLIOGRAPHY

Canby, Vincent. "Screen: Music of the 50s: 'Let the Good Times Roll' is Rock Revival Cast." *New York Times*. May 26, 1973.

Chalmers, Robert. "Legend: Little Richard." *British GQ*. March 29, 2012.

Charles "Bud" Penniman Obituary. *Macon Telegraph*. February 20, 1952.

Cohn, Nik. *Awopbopaloobop Alopbamboom The Golden Age of Rock*. New York: Grove Press, 2001.

Dalton, David. "Little Richard: Child of God." *Rolling Stone*. May 28, 1970.

"Drum Legend Charles Connor Keeps on Knockin'." *Goldmine*. November 13, 2009.

Dunlap, Stanley. "Here's Why Little Richard Said Macon is 'Better than Anywhere," *Macon.com*. December 5, 2017.

Ferdman, Brian. "Review of Little Richard—Live at the Toronto Peace Festival 1969." *Jambands.com*. March 27, 2009.

Gibbs, Vernon. "Little Richard and Solomon Burke: Sex & God & Rock & Roll." *Village Voice*. August 10, 1982.

Grimes, A.C. "The Untold Truth of Little Richard." *Grunge.com*. November 2, 2017.

Grow, Kory. "John Waters on Little Richard: 'He Was the First Punk. He was the First Everything," *Rolling Stone*. May 9, 2020.

Guralnick, Peter. *Sweet Soul Music: Rhythm and Blues and the Southern Dream of Freedom*. New York: Little, Brown, 1986.

Harrington, Richard. "'Awopbopaloobop' and 'Alopbamboom,' as Little Richard Himself Would Be (and Was) First to Admit." *Washington Post*. November 12, 1984.

Harris, June. "Little Richard: Gaumont Theatre, Watford: Richard is Dynamic." *Disc*. October 1963.

Heutmaker, Megan. "Keep A Knockin': Charles Connor, The Ponderosa." *Stomp. com*. September 27, 2017.

Holdship, Bill. "Little Richard: The Quasar Speaks!" *Creem*. January 1985.

Jagger, Juliette. "The Domino Effect: How One of Toronto's Most Iconic Rock Concerts Almost Never Happened." *Noisey*. April 13, 2015.

Jopling, Norman. "Little Richard, Duane Eddy, The Shirelles: The Regal, Edmonton, London." *Record Mirror*. November 16, 1963.

Kousouris, Abby. "Woman Seeks to Replace Confederate Statue in Downtown Macon With Little Richard." *13WMAZ.com*. February 3, 2019.

"Little Richard: A Living Legend In His Time." *KRLA Beat*. May 28, 1966.

Little Richard, All Rock 'n' Roll and Blues Studio Recordings, little-richard. oldgood.org/en/recs.html.

"Little Richard Forsakes Rock 'N' Roll for Preaching." United Press International, *Sarasota Herald-Tribune*. August 17, 1979.

"Little Richard," IMDB.com.

Dir. Philip Casson. *Little Richard: Portrait of a Legend*. Documentary. 1977.

"Little Richard Questionnaire." *Vanity Fair*. November, 2000.

"Macon Black Music Roots: How a Little Boy from Macon, Ga., Ascended to Rock 'n' Roll Throne." *Macon Telegraph*. February 1, 1987.

"Macon's Big Annual Homecoming Dance And Show Expecting To Draw Huge Crowd To Be Staged at Macon Auditorium Friday Night." *Macon Telegraph*. August 5, 1955.

Malone, Chris. "A Brief History of Little Richard Grappling With his Sexuality & Religion." *Billboard*. October 9, 2017.

McDermott, John. *Ultimate Hendrix: An Illustrated Encyclopedia of Live Concerts and Sessions*. New York: Backbeat Books, 2009.

"Meet Rock and Roll's Original Bad Boy, Larry Williams." *Goldmine Magazine*. October 10, 2013.

Melody Maker review, Little Richard "I Need Love" (Columbia). November 19, 1966.

Millar, Bill. "Little Richard: Saville Theatre, London." *Soul Music Monthly*. March 1967.

Payne, Jim. "Little Richard: The Explosive Little Richard." *Crawdaddy!*. May 1967.

Ribowsky, Mark. *Dreams to Remember: Otis Redding, Stax Records, and the Transformation of Southern Soul*. New York: Liveright, 2017.

Roby, Steven and Brad Schreiber. *Becoming Jimi Hendrix*. New York: DaCapo Press, 2010.

"Rock 'n' Roll Pioneer Little Richard's $118 Million Lawsuit." United Press International. November 27, 1984.

Sullivan, Jim. "Rock Poet Richard Hell Finds Some Solace." *Boston Globe*. November 6, 1982.

Takiff, Jonathan. "Joni Mitchell Ran Offstage Crying, Little Richard Brought the House Down: Why Doesn't Anyone Remember the Atlantic City Pop Festival?" *Philadelphia Inquirer*. July 28, 2019.

"The Fabulous Little Richard." *Macon Telegraph*. December 12, 1954.

"The Rise and Fall of Vee-Jay Records." *NPR: Fresh Air*. January 15, 2008.

Waters, John. "When John Waters Met Little Richard." *The Guardian*. November 27, 2010.

Wexler, Jerry and David Ritz. *Rhythm and the Blues: A Life in American Music*. New York: St. Martin's Press, 1993.

INDEX

ABOUT THE AUTHOR

MARK RIBOWSKY is the *New York Times* acclaimed author of *The Supremes: A Saga of Motown Dreams, Success, and Betrayal*; *He's a Rebel: Phil Spector—Rock and Roll's Legendary Producer*; *Don't Look Back: Satchel Paige in the Shadows of Baseball*; and *Signed, Sealed, Delivered: The Soulful Journey of Stevie Wonder*. He has written for *SPORT* magazine and *Inside Sports*, *TV Guide*, *Playboy*, and *Penthouse*. Ribowsky has appeared on *Dateline NBC*, *Primetime Live* (ABC), *Connie Chung*, *Geraldo Rivera*, *The Tavis Smiley Show*, and many other network and cable TV shows. He lives in Boca Raton, Florida.